AND GOD SAID!

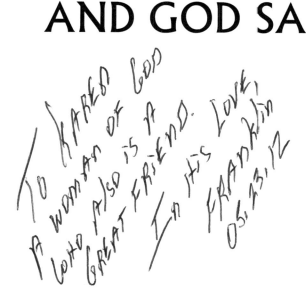

FRANKLIN A. ALVEY, PH.D., TH.D.

iUniverse, Inc.
Bloomington

AND GOD SAID!

Copyright © 2011 by Franklin A. Alvey, Ph.D., Th.D.

All rights reserved. No part of this book may be used or reproduced by any means, graphic, electronic, or mechanical, including photocopying, recording, taping or by any information storage retrieval system without the written permission of the publisher except in the case of brief quotations embodied in critical articles and reviews.

iUniverse books may be ordered through booksellers or by contacting:

iUniverse
1663 Liberty Drive
Bloomington, IN 47403
www.iuniverse.com
1-800-Authors (1-800-288-4677)

Because of the dynamic nature of the Internet, any web addresses or links contained in this book may have changed since publication and may no longer be valid. The views expressed in this work are solely those of the author and do not necessarily reflect the views of the publisher, and the publisher hereby disclaims any responsibility for them.

Any people depicted in stock imagery provided by Thinkstock are models, and such images are being used for illustrative purposes only.
Certain stock imagery © Thinkstock.

ISBN: 978-1-4620-3759-9 (sc)
ISBN: 978-1-4620-3760-5 (ebk)

Library of Congress Control Number: 2011912576

Printed in the United States of America

iUniverse rev. date: 08/17/2011

"He has already won the battle you are currently in.
Stop fighting the war and rest in Him."

Bishop C. T. Wells

*To my wife, Barbara Jean Blom-Alvey, the bravest person I have ever known.
"A better Marine was she than I."*

FOREWORD

All of us face hardship in our lives, but not all of us come through such times with stronger faith and a compelling testimony to the grace of God. You're holding a book that deals with the harsh realities of sin in the world, and the glorious truth of God's presence, provision, and purposes.

Dr. Franklin Alvey speaks and writes like a statesman. His marriage to Barbara for well over 50 years and his walk with Christ for even longer makes him a seasoned voice. More importantly, he has experienced "Wit's End" more than once—through bankruptcy, poverty, life-threatening illness, and more—and learned the sound of the Master's voice and the blessing of obedience. This book shares some of that journey and some of the important biblical principles that have sustained the Alvey's over the decades.

I'm honored to write the foreword to this wonderfully personal book. I'm enriched by the faithfulness of the Alvey's as they have resisted the temptation to worship at the altar of materialism that our culture esteems so highly. But Franklin Alvey is not the hero of the story. The book points consistently and clearly to Christ and affirms the incredible and life-changing power of the Son of God when we yield to Him.

As you read, it may feel a little like sitting around the campfire with a tribal elder. Listen carefully. Hear the wisdom. Consider the truths. And respond with the same faith in Christ that has become the guiding light of the Alvey's life. May the Lord grant you joy, peace, and revelation as you read. Because of grace.

David Timms, Ph.D.
William Jessup University

"LORD, WHAT AM I GOING TO DO?"

> *"I will be his Father, and he shall be my son. If he commit iniquity, I will chasten him with the rod of men, and with the stripes of the children of men. But my mercy shall not depart away from him . . . ."*
>
> II Samuel 7: 14-15

We hope the testimony of our life's experience as a married couple, now approaching 53 years together, will represent a benefit to those who currently may be going through their own "Wit's End." We've added warning signs that have the capacities to induce Spiritual incarceration, as well as our antidote for maintaining sanity during mental upheavals caused by an out of control life. Reading on, you'll see that we have been to the bottom of the pit and miraculously survived by the grace of Him who tested us. Yes, that is correct. He will allow us to be tested!

Our own cycle of trials has opened our eyes to what's happening to our world. Our Lord has made us very aware, due to our inordinate bouts of pain, as to what's happening around us. It's almost like The Holy Spirit allowed us to go through these calamities so as to make us aware of things to come. Or, if you're a prisoner of war you are made keenly aware of those who have it far worse than you within the dungeon walls called your domain.

So, what is Wit's End which strikes everyone irrespective of income nationality or place in society? Job stress, financial woes, family complications, illness, weariness, anxiety, addictive disorders such as alcoholism, gambling or simply tired of going on—to include suicide—can all be defined as harmful physical and emotional situations which occur when the requirements of the current situation one's involved with does not match the capabilities, resources, or strength so as to balance the bad with the good.

A clear picture of out of control Wit's End can be compared to that of a World War II B-17E Flying Fortress Bomber over Germany, in 1944, whose aircraft structure has been hit innumerable number of times by a number of Germany's infamous Messerschmitt ME-109 fighter planes to the point that all hydraulic controls are inoperable. On top of this two of its four engines have been shot away while the third is afire. The pilot can no longer control the airplane. It soon starts a spiral nosedive straight to Mother Earth at over 300 miles per hour. On fire, and out of control, the pilot is frantic—screaming in hopelessness—in attempting to maintain the aircraft's controls while the co-pilot sits dead; still strapped in his chair. Other than the pilot, only two of the eleven crew members remain alive. As the aircraft plummets in a head first dive, the men attempt to reach an exit hatch only to be held back by the craft's pitch accompanied by loose equipment and dead comrades clogging the pathway leading to the only door to freedom. You know how this story ends.

Why expose this particular picture? Because every day—in our country especially now—millions of Americans feel as helpless and out of control as these imaginary airmen in a failing bomber only seconds away from its final resting place.

"They [voluntarily] go down to the seas in ships, that do business in great waters, these are the works of The Lord, and His wonders in the deep. He commands, and raises the stormy wind, which lifts up the waves thereof. They mount up to heaven, they go down again to the depths: their soul is melted because of [fear] trouble. They reel to and fro, and stagger like drunken men, and are at their

Wit's End." Psalm 107: 23-27 [Italics mine]

WHEN THE CHALLENGE MORPHS INTO A BRICK WALL

The concept of wit's end [extreme stress] is sometimes confused with challenges. We must not mix the two. Completing a challenge successfully is a feeling of satisfaction. Take the NFL running back. When he is responsible for making the touchdown, the challenge is met. This is why controlled challenges are an important ingredient for health and success be it sports or business. There is always a little stress associated with competition. Just ask the collegiate or professional NCAA/NBA/WNBA basketball player, after getting knocked sideways a half a dozen times, if they had any challenges before scoring their two points? This is why challenges are good providing that we are making headway . . . . providing we are in control. It is only when the challenge morphs into a brick wall or an impassable situation that Wit's End moves in with an attempt to take control.

If you are saved through Christ and truly walking with Him, the Holy Spirit will always advise you at the outset of a current challenge that is not satisfactory with Him. Conversely, He will advise you if you're on the right track. These are key issues in avoiding these attacks.

> *If you've been walking with Our Lord for an inordinate period of time you should therefore be in control of those situations*

that may be causing you "Wit's Ends." Conversely, there are [more than not] Christians who have been saved for many years—to include Pastors, elders, Sunday school teachers and the like—who are still no closer to God than they were the day of salvation. Having both feet planted firmly in the world simply represents never having taken a closer walk with Him. Simply put, some of the "old man" still hangs on disrupting the Saints' walk every time a Spiritual shot is fired. This need not be!

I have lined up seven items representing traumatic situations that are sure to create situations involving Wit's End. There are obviously more. Irrespective, these are some of the more popular sand pits.

SEVEN THAT WILL TURN INTO A MENTAL TSUNAMI

[1] So, you're about: to enter a marriage agreement not sanctified by Our Lord. He/she, that is the person you're about to marry, is not saved. However, you're just "sure" everything will turn out OK because you are so much in love.

[2] Borrowing money from the wrong person at the wrong time including the fact that you really do not know how these funds will be repaid. Viz. Substandard mortgage.

[3] Quitting a job "without His permission," just because you're dissatisfied, when you have nowhere else to go.

[4] Holding a grudge against a fellow Christian when you know better.

[5] Grieving the Holy Spirit by entering into a business situation, or job, displeasing to Him.

[6] A mind reeling with fear of man, fear of the unknown, lust, fornication, vanity, pride, surfeiting, destructive thoughts and foul language.

[7] Creating apostasy against Our Lord.

> *"I begin by saying that our history will be what we make it to be. If we go as we are, and history takes its revenge, retribution will not limp in catching up with us."*
> Edward R. Morrow—CBS Anchor
> 1954
> From the Movie "Good Night and Good Luck"
> Directed by George Clooney

OUT OF HARMONY WITH GOD

In past years I've always known when that particular business transaction I was about to take on was out of harmony with our Lord. At that time I did know better. You see, I didn't pray about it. I did not seek His will or thoughts! I pressed on anyway as I felt "I" could straighten out the mess I created and still make money. I wasn't feckless; I simply desired to remain successful while feeding my family.

Nevertheless, each day after the ink was dry on the initiated agreement, Franklin awoke to the pain and discomfort due to a thorny association with the incorrect business concept. I knew I was on the wrong road. Our Lord was talking to me about the mess I had produced. He would say, "Franklin, I did warn you. You were aware of my displeasure when you initiated this agreement. I attempted to warn you that this procedure would not work. Also Franklin, what about the stress you are placing on your wife? You did not think of the pressure your error would bring upon Barbara. Now she also suffers because of your selfishness. When you made this decision you left me, as well as your wife, out of the picture for the sake of personal gain." Now the only choice I had was to ride it out until the Lord rescued me. Sometimes this took months. Other times it took years of tears and pain while I waited for him to remove me from this problematical discomfort that I created. I didn't listen to His warnings! No, I was never involved in anything illicit. That does not matter. If you're on the wrong road—in attempting a Spiritual association with Our Lord—you are on the incorrect path. What was my MO as a senior manager? I was a hands-on guy who had a tendency to remove the very oxygen from the room when I exercised my zealousness.

I am reminded of my former flights of despair through Deuteronomy 1:31-33 *"And in the desert, there you saw how the Lord your God carried you as a parent carries their child. He carried you where ever you went until you came to this place. (32) In spite of this you did not trust the Lord your God. (33) Who went ahead of you to find places to camp? He appeared in a column of fire at night and a column of smoke during the day to show you which route to take." (RSV)*

God chose the camps for his people all along the way from the time they left Egypt until the time they entered the Promised Land. Not only this, He also provided provisions of food and water making sure they were well taken care of as long as they followed his law.

The columns of fire at night and smoke during the day are no more. In its place is the leading via our Jesus Christ through the Holy Spirit which is the substitute of the original Mosaic Law. If we listen carefully, He will speak to us in the same way he spoke to the Israelites in the desert while they trooped onward to the Promised Land. We will be able to comprehend His direction providing our ears are not stuffed full of ourselves making it impossible for His word to penetrate our soul. If there is too much of me in the way—disallowing Him entrance to my spirit—the only voice I'll hear is my own. Being a soul man is deadly!

SPIRITUAL POINTERS THE ALVEY'S HAVE LEARNED THROUGH TRIAL AND ERROR

I must separate myself from my [feelings] soul. I cannot allow my emotion to lead me no matter how difficult the current situation is that I am facing. *I must turn any serious matter over to Him and leave it there.*

Set values as to where I want to go in God. Make sure that they are secure and approved by Him before making a judgment call. We'll talk more in this issue later when we approach goal setting.

Envision, through my plans, what God has in store for my future. Eliminate distractions. Ask him for advice while en route. Maintain a Christian attitude at all times. He'll do a proper job of leading you through every storm.

Understand that arriving at my destination, on my own, is out of the question. If He leads He deserves the credit! I will always need his help and support. As long as I meditate on him I am safe. Be aware of the enemy's continuous attempt of sidetracking your efforts.

Remember that our Lord never leads via conventional wisdom. This means he'll come to you through the coffee pot versus the front door. *Also underlined that He expects us to put up with certain bouts of discomfort while en route—this is part of the process called the learning of patience through training.*

We must be and/or remain saved and anointed so that our [again] inner ear can clearly distinguish as to what the Holy Spirit is saying to us before any plans come to fruition.

Never, ever, ever enter into a legal permanent agreement without first going to Our Lord for permission. Do not make a move until He sanctifies the relationship even if it takes weeks, months and yes even years before your spirit receives a yes or no. If, in the meantime, the other party decides not to wait for your decision and runs on;

then you will have received your answer. He will make it up to you by delivering a far better issue, on your behalf, than the former on down the line.

The unsaved or fallen away need not apply for his help during an exercise of this nature. These issues are only available to those who have said, "Lord, please come into my heart. I am tired of doing this alone. I need your help. Please save me."

> "Sorrow is a valid emotion—part of the richness of life. Therefore, feel it and endure it, but do not allow melancholy to define you."
>
> Abraham Lincoln

IT WILL DO NO GOOD TO HOWL.

I have learned during my 64 years [out of 78] of walking with our Lord that he will continue to keep me in a "Wit's End" situation until I have learned to trust Him completely no matter how much distaste I find myself in. It does not matter how hopeless my future seems to be at the time of my trial. Sometimes I simply do not know the answer. However, staying with Him—no matter the pain—was a lesson well worth the time and energy. I always remembered that I was a soldier. I volunteered for His army therefore He expected me [That is Barbara and Franklin] to push on in His name with the understanding that wisdom and revelation are the only factors associated with the knowledge of God. I have learned to follow hard after the words of Jeremiah.

> "And it shall come to pass, 'after I have plucked them out' I will return, and have compassion on them, and will bring them again, every man to his heritage and every man to his land."
>
> Jeremiah 12:15 KJV

THEY DID NOT LEARN THEN. CAN WE LEARN NOW?

We see this hopeless and distrustful attitude happen time after time with the children of Israel in the wilderness. They were always howling and complaining against Moses and the law. Again and again God brought them to a position of Wit's End so as to test them, to see if they would trust him. But each time they failed. Here are some examples.

First, immediately after departing Egypt, the Lord brought them to a place called

Pihahioth, between Migdol and the sea. He had shut them in—the sea in front—with mountains on both sides, and Pharaoh coming up behind them. God had actually led them to a place of human hopelessness—a place called Wit's End. All he wanted from the Israelites was a simple statement of trust. He wanted them to say we know our God will deliver us no matter what the enemy sets before us.

If you panic at Wit's End as Israel did—fainting, accusing God of not caring—he nevertheless will move at the last moment and deliver you. But, afterwards, you can be absolutely sure that He will take you right back to another Wit's End experience—because you did not come through the last one trusting him.

[The oncoming world calamity will produce mega-boat loads of Christian people caught up in the worst kind of Wit's End.]

Indeed, just three days after their Red Sea deliverance, Israel was back in the middle of multiple crises. The people—as well as their animals—were hot, exhausted and overcome by thirst. The Israeli scouts came back crying, "There is water ahead at Marah, however, we cannot drink it—it's sour!"

WE DESIRE RETURNING TO EGYPT!

Did you really ever consider why the Israelites clambered so much about returning to a land where, if they did reenter Egypt again, they would be enslaved perhaps indefinitely? There is an actual reason, regarding their complaint, which I always specifically sought after. Here it is:

Alfred Edersheim (1825-1889) of Jewish parents then, converted to Christianity at an early age through a Scottish Presbyterian chaplain, studied theology at Edinburgh and Berlin. He taught at Oxford University from 1884 until his death. From his book BIBLE HISTORY, [Hendrickson Publishers, 1006 pages—previously in seven volumes] Professor Edersheim wrote the following of his Jewish descendents as to their reason for such lust after the country that had bound them as slaves for hundreds of years

"About the middle of August, the red, turbid waters of the rising [Nile] river are distributed by canals over the country, and carry fruitfulness with them. On receding, the Nile leaves behind it a thick red soil, which its waters had carried from Central Africa, and over this rich deposit the seed is sown. Rain? There is none, nor is there need for it to fertilize the land. The Nile also furnishes the most pleasant and even nourishing water for 'drinking.' And some physicians have ascribed to it having healing virtues. It is scarcely necessary to add that the river teems with fish. Luxuriously rich and green, amidst surrounding desolation, the banks of the Nile and its numerous canals are like a well watered garden under a tropical sky. Where climate and soil are the best conceivable, the fertility must be unparalleled. The ancient Egyptians seem to have also bestowed great attention on their fruit and flower gardens, which like ours, were attached to their villas. On the monuments we see gardeners presenting handsome bouquets; gardens traversed by alleys and adorned with pavilions and colonnades; orchards stocked with palms, figs, pomegranates, citrons, oranges, plums, mulberries, apricots, etc. While in the vineyards, as in Italy, the vines were trained to meet across wooden rods and hung down in rich festoons.

Such was [*not so*] in the desolate dreariness and famine of the wilderness. Israel was tempted [and complained]. Their later reminiscences of Egypt accord with this view. In the wilderness they looked back with sinful longing to the time when they had cast their nets into the Nile, and drawn them in weighted with fish; and when their gardens and fields, by the waterside, had yielded rich crops—'the cucumbers, and the melons, and the leeks and the onions, and the garlick.' (Numb. 11:5)." [Italics mine]

> Bible History by Professor Alfred Eldersheim Copyright 1995 by Hendrickson Publishers, Peabody Massachusetts. Used by permission. 1006 pages; all rights reserved. First printing 1876-1887.

They became so blind with lust for a life of slavery that they forgot—and didn't care—what The Lord had in mind for them. [Do you]?

Our 21st century man still follows the same pattern. Many Christians find themselves mired in an emotional pool of quicksand. They want the problems resolvesd IMMEDIATELY. Too many times we ignore the Lord's leading of waiting until He provides the escape route. If we do not wait on Him the chances are very good that we'll find we've returned to the same pool of vomit from which we hastened to escape from.

It is interesting to point out here that Franklin knew well the lessons learned from not waiting on our Lord.

UNTIL YOU SAY YES LORD!

Do you see the pattern here? If Franklin does not learn to trust Him, in simple childlike faith during periods of testing, he will bring him back around the mountain again and again because I complained about my circumstances or yearned for something that was not His will. I'll go from this test to still another—and onto another until I have learned to trust our God. <u>Some of us never learn to trust Him during an entire lifetime. At death's door many are in the middle of a Wit's End crisis—still struggling to get out.</u> If this be so your life it is full of misery, discomfort and unhappiness. You will maintain this lifestyle until your last breath. Or, until you say "yes Lord!" Wasted years, wasted life!

Scripture makes it very clear. It wasn't Satan who led Israel to this testing place. It was the cloud, God himself, which had brought them to this point. Once more, the people were at Wit's End—what an awful accusation against Moses and the God of Abraham. They said, "Moses, you brought us here to die." Statements of this nature smack of self-centeredness or out of control selfishness.

We are now into the 21st century and man's attitude has never changed since the days of Mosaic Law. Saints still complain and accuse God of not caring. They do so without examining themselves carefully so as to find out why they are so unhappy. Or, they do not carefully study the Book of The Law so as to examine how and why Adam and Eve gave our Spiritual inheritance away and in its place opened the way for Pandora's Box to encompass "all of us if we allow."

Nevertheless, God knows exactly what to do about your problem. He knows the precise hour that he will deliver you. All he wants from you is quiet trust. He wants you to confess, "My God is with me. He knows the way out of my dilemma."

Short lived situations representing infrequent episodes of Wit's End chapters pose little risk. However many times these challenges become unresolved and elongated because you did not do your part. This is when the body can be kept in a constant state of aggravation which increases the wear and tear on its biological system. If you allow this situation to go unchecked, permanent fatigue or physical damage could result affecting the body's ability to repair and defend itself. In essence, you can become seriously compromised. As a result, the risk of inordinate injury or disease escalates as during prolonged stretches of stress the body automatically releases an imbalanced chemical reaction which disjoints the bodily functions. When extreme stress sets in, your sympathetic nervous system assumes control of your reflexes. You may make decisions—based on survival—which you could come to regret at a later date—sometimes too late. It is an extremely serious matter.

Is it any wonder hospital beds are overflowing with patients necessitating drugs which will hopefully put them back together? Yet all too often their physician is at a loss as to the prognosis. Neither doctor nor [blind to the problem] patient is aware of the cause and effect.

I have, as a pastor, made many visits to the hospital bedside of well known Christians who were bound by out of control nerve endings. Their reason for bed rest is caused by not turning the problems and challenges of life's situations over to Our Lord. I have known many to pass into the next life prematurely due to being overcome by Wit's End.

My wife and I have had tremendous compassion for those in the US who have lost their homes to fire and floods, tornados, cyclones and current financial disasters. [The great financial bailout!] Some, who have lost only their worldly possessions, will confess that it was devastating but thank God the family is intact which means they'll be able to rebuild while others buckle under the pressure creating an element of despair which in them produces a Wit's End situation beyond comprehension. Some of these people never pull out of the nose dive.

This is why so many individuals, who fall, are unable to rebound. They can eventually attract cardiovascular diseases, muscle disorders causing skeletal distortions, psychological maladies that create mental or physical workplace injury. In many cases, premature death follows.

"We're all put to the test. But it never comes at the point that we prefer."

Anthony Hopkins
From the movie, "The Edge."

Over the length of our 52 plus years of marriage we have, as previously mentioned, encountered some difficult quicksand beds. Some of these situations brought us to our knees. In some instances we lost everything right down to the furniture. However, after the first two or three major trials we commenced to believe [totally] in our Lord Jesus and His promises to keep us. The following is a solid example.

> *David wrote, "Before I was afflicted I went astray: but now I have kept thy word . . . . It is good for me that I have been afflicted; that I might learn [His] thy statues." Psalm 119: 67 & 70. KJV [Italics mine]*

Barbara and I counted on each other to push on, irrespective our pain, including the faith in our Lord's ability to overcome seemingly impossible obstacles. This enabled us to hang on so as to build a better life through, at times, back to back bone jarring Wit's End tribulations. We were under the impression at times that we would never get out from under the crush. What was our learning process? We used previous platforms of His miracles—as spiritual flotation devices to lean on during the storms—so as to build a new horizon. That is, we were able to beat the previously stacked odds against us due to a recorded history of successes through Him. So, when the next horrendous trial entered our camp we used the courage gained from the previous difficulty as a reminder that we can win this one, through Him, too. Hard? Yes! Impossible? No, as Our Lord was always with us. He will also be with you if you believe. This is how we successfully manage today.

It would have been wonderful if we had known His recipes for success when first married. As we all know, it likely does not work that way.

Some Christians think that once saved means a wall of Teflon surrounds their mind thus keeping back any complication, illness or challenge. In reality just the opposite is true. Once saved the enemy sends his ravaging satanic dogs—to chase, maim and hurt—in an attempt to pull the new convert down forcing an attitude of surrender. In some cases new believers may turn back to the old ways of life [sin] as it seems easier than fighting. That's fine until one day, due to your never fully accepting Christ, you fall into the pit of hell lost forever with no way to escape. When that takes place "Wit's End" lasts forever.

SO WHY DO WE WRITE?

This is not a medical book. It is simply a testimony on how we continued to overcome some of the worst of life's situations so as to run on and see what the end has in store for us. Our writing is hopefully a warning of things to come. This is a book of helps.

Also, this reading is not a book containing a punch line at the end on how to make money. We're not going to ask you to send the Alveys money enabling you to gain access to happiness forever by the reading of these words.

It is a writing dedicated to helping those to overcome afflicted situations from the eyes of two people who lost "everything" more than once and yet, through trial and error, were able to rebound as we believed in each other through the Christ who saved us. Our many trials have produced a wisdom and knowledge, leading to survival regarding the futuristic tough economic times which are surely now in transit to many. No amount of money, world armies or global economic power will stop what is about to take place in and through our world economy. Such is commencing as these words are being penned. We'll discuss more on this segment later.

My wife and I have contemplated writing our experiences and recommendations for over 20 years. It's delay has been held up by a myriad of obstacles connected with the raising of our children, career growth, time needed to maintain our health along with the ongoing battle in combating our own life's "Wit's End."

Some these periods were filled with uncertainty. We seemingly proceeded in a fog so thick that we were barely able to make out our life's compass reading which we were hoping would lead us out of the furnace of disparagement and affliction. We did not realize it at the time of our trials however we were being led on a route that took us through many avenues of training—a school of learning spiritual warfare—we did not know where the trail led. We did know that Our Lord was guiding. How did we know this? Because no matter how devastating the trial He kept us from being thrown in the street. Further, there were times, on any given day, that we had no money. I mean none! The next day, through some quirk (miracle) a check would arrive in the mail covering our needs for that moment. It was that way for three or four consecutive years.

A HERO SHE IS:

As this time my wife Barbara is entering her eleventh year of remission represented by two types of cancer being Non Hodgkin's Lymphoma and carcinoma of the lungs which have taken a serious toll on her life following two horrific operations only three days apart. She died at completion of the second operation and miraculously regained consciousness through the expert hands of the hospital's nurses. Yet through all of this Barbara has remained stoic to the point of never complaining followed by continued Praise to Our Lord believing that He will touch her enabling a total cure. I also know that she will be healed! Even today, after all this time, she is still bed ridden with pain and nausea. However, currents medical tests reveal her cancers receding to the point that her health is returning to normal. There is a lesson to her pain. She will futuristically be more than qualified—through this test—to comfort other women pocked with incurable diseases. She stood on Psalms 42:11 *"Why are thou cast down, O my soul? And why art thou disquieted within me? Who is the health of my countenance and my God? [I will praise Him evermore]"* [Italics mine]

When you ask Barbara if she laments over her physical trials her answer revolves around II Corinthians 4:17. And he said,

"Our light affliction, which is but for a moment, works for us a far more exceeding and eternal weight of glory." KJV

> *"Out of the presses of pain cometh the soul's best wine*
> *And the eyes that have shed no rain can shed but little shine."*
> Don't Waste Your Sorrows
> By Paul E. Billheimer
> A Christian Literature Publication
> By Permission

Franklin spent three very tough years in the US Marine Corps during the Korean Campaign as a member of 3rd Marine Division Force Recon Special Forces where he received his share of decorations which are not important here. However, Barbara is a better Marine than this writer ever thought possible. Barbara, as her many friends will attest, is such a loving and caring person. She never desires anyone harm. This includes the most heathen individuals. You might think a person of her nature would be surrounded by protectionism from Our Lord since she displays all the attributes of true Christianity.

Bringing you up to date: As of December 2008 Barbara had another CT scan. The prognosis was not good. Her medical physician advised that her cancers had "jumped the fire line" and were now spreading. As of March 16, 2009, Barbara entered into a third radical surgery in an attempt to remove a carcinoma from her lung. As of this writing she continues to battle forward in her healing process.

We do not know what the final outcome will be. Franklin does know this. Barbara has turned her physical trial completely over to Him and is at peace with her condition. We both believe, in spite of the seemingly one sided obstacles, that Our Lord will heal her.

Our Senior Pastor, Bishop C.T. Wells, has taught us the three methods associated with gaining mastery over such evilness as sickness and disease which is having a marvelous effect relative to our prayer requests for Barbara. These are based on [A] Isaiah 1:19 <u>*CLAIM*</u> the goodness of God; [B] Luke 10:19 <u>*BIND*</u> the enemy and cast him back into hell and [C] Hebrews 1:7 and 14 which is <u>*COMMAND*</u> God's angels to now come and heal since the enemy has been evicted.

There are a bevy of wonderful people, totally immersed in Christ, who have penned a number of books on apologetics relative to sickness and disease. They explain and describe Saints who—totally in love with Christ—suffer endlessly, some for a lifetime. They attempt to outline the reasons for such pain.

I am one of the many who do not understand why some of the most courageous and brave people endure such persecution. I have visited many sick folk in homes and hospitals and have always been drawn to such humility. Many are, without a doubt, the greatest witnesses for Our Lord. One of those is Barbara Jean Blom Alvey. Biblically based knowledge escapes me as to why so many of the best suffer so much. So many of the worst cases bring tears when they say, "Doctor Franklin, I am praying for you and your family." Such reverence to Him! I have drawn great testimonies from these heroes of faith who have increased my belief.

Another trial has come as a result of Barbara's multiple surgeries is the loss of her Executive Assistant position, to the

President of a major hospitality company, which has caused great financial hardship on the family. Irrespective, He continues to meet our needs.

Someday, when we get to the other side, I'm convinced I'll have the opportunity to meet many of these champions of faith. I never question God on these issues. Rather I look to Him for assurance that these wonders of faith are in His hands. Then, I also must remember that the Bible clearly teaches that *That ye may be the children of your Father which is in heaven: for he makes his sun to rise on the evil and good, and sends rain on the just and unjust,*
Matthew 5:45 KJV

How does a mere mortal challenge and question Him that made the entire world and all of its inhabitants including the entire universe?

SOME OF YOU ARE IN TRAINING

Some of you are going through a Wit's End situation because you asked for it. That is, somewhere you made a request to Our Lord pertaining to your faith. You said through some phraseology of prayer—to Him—that you desired to be a better person. You wanted to lose some of the excess baggage relative to fear of man, fear of the unknown, lust, fornication, bad temper, alcohol or drug addition, adultery, selfishness, deceit and possibly a whole lot more. The Lord said OK! I will do this for you which will ultimately draw you closer to me. However, this may alter your personality as you are deeply entrenched in some of these [sins] habits. This will take time. However, together—if you'll trust the Holy Spirit—He will bring you out. Many times, at this point, the trials, pain or Wit's End situations commence. Why? You are in spiritual withdrawal.

Here is an example. You are a selfish and vain person. Your thoughts and actions mainly focus on you. You live—in some cases—under the rule of conditional love. That is, make me happy and I will like you. Do something that annoys me and I'll shut you out. Or, your self confidence is nil and none. You have lived with a negative condition for so long that depression almost becomes your middle name. You simply do not have faith in yourself. You believe God; however you do not believe in Him. Here's an example on how He may heal you.

The Lord, so as to test you, shuts down your job. You're out of work. Money becomes slim to none. If one reverts to his old self—during this jobless period—you'll pout and feel sorry for yourself. You may cut yourself off from seeing friends and acquaintances. You are miserable as that pack on your back called "self." If on the other hand you believes that God will answer your request and bring you out you'll praise God during this time focusing on Him to bring a new employer into view. You'll wait it out no matter the length of time it takes to secure a new position. Always . . . under these circumstances The Lord cares for his people. Therefore the pain is shifted from you onto the Holy Spirit.

This test, of being thrown into Wit's End, may fall under a cornucopia of situations. Viz., living with a contemptuous faithless person; falling into bankruptcy; sickness; extreme chemistry imbalance with another person; living with an ungrateful, contemptuous, wayward son or daughter, a son or daughter who committed suicide causing you to grieve thinking that you should have done something to resolve the issue, etc. It doesn't matter.

Here however is the key issue behind this teat. *If you fail this test you will have wasted your sorrow. Yielding to self-pity, depression and rebellion is a waste of sorrow. Franklin—or anyone else—who has unsuccessfully sought healing through Christ and yet still submits to resentment, discontent, impatience and bitterness against God are wasting what God intended for growth, and love through a Christ-like maturity If He chastened the Israelites for unbelief will He not provide the same for Franklin?* IBID

Remember, what happened [is happening] to you was sanctioned by Our Lord. [Has thou considered my servant Franklin?] If I fail this test Our Lord will take me around the same mountain repeatedly until I have learned my lesson. After all, didn't I ask Him to heal me?

THE ALVEY'S LITANY

Anything you've have read thus far has little comprehension unless you read and fathomed some of the underlining situations we went through as a couple. For your observation, listed below is a brief history of the Wit's End embattlements we encountered and eventually overcame. This is not the entire list. We thought we would only itemize those battles representing some of the most difficult times within our married career. They are as follows:

1. 1959 Barbara's family is totally against her marrying Franklin. It becomes so heated that Barbara and Franklin threatened to elope. They desired Barbara marrying someone far more deftly suave and persuasively pleasing. Now, however, the entire family is as close as air is to water.

2. 1959-1962 Barbara has two miscarriages.

3. 1963 The death of our daughter Kimberly.

4. 1971 Barbara spends six weeks in a cancer hospital diagnosed with lymphatic disease. (The cancer starts here then rests)

5. 1979 Franklin spends 5 months in the unemployment rolls. [Specific reason exists here which is God induced which commenced in 1969. I would rather explain this time of our lives through verbal testimony as pictures, through words, connect more effectively than black and white on paper.]

6. 1983 Continued financial disasters cause the loss of our 3000 square foot home in Lake Oswego which also includes 100% of all furnishings. From there we move

into a rented 400 square foot, cockroach infested, furnished apartment where the 24/7 smell of beer [downtown brewery] fermentation was unbearable. We were on the wrong side of town with only our clothes as an asset. This was a long way down from beautiful Lake Oswego. Overnight all we have worked for had vanished. A key poignant issue at this point is that during these horrendous financial trials was the period that Barbara wrote some of her most beautiful music of praise and worship.

7. 1984 Franklin is once again on the unemployment rolls for 10 months. We lived on hamburger helper, hamburger helper and hamburger helper. We never informed anyone of our plight as we felt it was God's

job to bring us out—not man's money. As a consequence of this unemployment we were forced to file for bankruptcy in 1991. This was one of our major disasters.

8. In 1985 Franklin carried the *Oregonian* newspaper for 19 months seven days weekly (335 papers) to help make ends meet. Up at 11:30PM for Bible study for 30 minutes then onto "The Shack" or newspaper pick-up station. Finished by 06:30 in time for work.

9. 2001 Barbara is again diagnosed with Non-Hodgkin's lymphoma which is now spreading. This is followed by major surgery and chemotherapy.

10. 2007 Barbara is diagnosed with lung cancer.

11. 2007 Barbara has two back-to-back major surgeries to remove portions of her right lung tissue and one third of her lower lung. Post systems include constant nausea and vomiting for 18 months which is lessoning. As of this writing she has been battling cancer for eleven years. She was in remission until her December 2008 examination which disclosed that her cancers were again spreading.

12. 2009 Barbara once again has lung cancer surgery. This time on her left lung to remove a carcinoma. Post systems include much pain

and nausea which still plague her. As of this writing she has been battling cancer for 11 years.

CHECKING THE ATTITUDE

What is our attitude, towards our Lord, after facing so many years of trials? We are both better people for these battles. After looking back on these turmoil's we still Praise Him who allowed us to go through these very painful engagements as it taught us the lessons He desired of us which included patience and especially the building of faith in Him. We could have said, "Lord, why haven't you interceded on our behalf. You have put more on us that we can bear." We never assumed an attitude of this nature. Yes, we were broken hearted; yes we wept together. However we knew—in the long run—that He would pull us out. Here is a substantial miracle for your observation.

No one ever—including our immediate family to include our Church members—knew of our financial difficulties. We kept the entire subject matter buttoned up between the Lord and ourselves including not calling our relatives or friends so as to seek financial aid. Additionally, we continued to pay our Church tithes and offerings as we knew this was one of the areas representing a way out. Paying tithes—in time of great stress—is a hallmark of faith. We felt He would want it that way as in the end He received the glory by rescuing us which He did. Were we disciplined people? Yes we were. The discipline did not come as a result of our trials. We were, as business people, always disciplined. This helped a great deal. Our motto, during so many trying months was "Get it done."

"Because we have sought The Lord our God, we have sought Him, and He has given us rest on every side."
                II Chronicles 14:7 KJV

FRONTLINE BATTLES

Before we get to the antidote of recommended survival modes let's describe some situations that represent life's logical frontline battles.

As previously stated the synonym of Wit's End is stress. Everyone, at one time or another, has an abundant supply of this paralytic. Stress is necessary for one's survival. It's part of feeling your way through the jungle of life. Without stress you wouldn't know when to say stop, or, I've had enough, slow down.

I believe it a poignant period to interject a little Bible 101 as to what really allowed Wit's End to proliferate in the first place.

The following excerpt is taken from "Death and the Afterlife" by Dr. Robert A. Morey. He paints—what I would call—a perfect picture.

> *"On the day that man sinned in the Garden of Eden, he "died," i.e., he was separated and alienated from the person and 'gifts' of God. This alienation let to conscious fear, [Wit's End] anxiety, guilt and remorse (Gen.3:7, 10) God's first punishment for sin not only included mental suffering and a guilty conscience, but also physical suffering, as they would have to wear clothing against the cold, obtain food by the sweat of their brow, and experience pain in childbirth (Gen 3:16-24) Divine punishment for Adam*

and Eve did not mean annihilation, but mental and physical suffering."

Here, as an example, is a perfect analogy. Suppose you're warming yourself next this large campfire in the woods during sub-zero weather? You can only get so close without burning yourself. Your senses say be warmed not burned. These are your automatic mechanisms advising you to stand back. Yet, sometimes we not only get too close, we actually catch on fire. When this occurs we're now into a full blown case of out of control stress or "Wit's End" in attempting to extinguish the fire which signifies that we can't rid ourselves of the dilemma until the fire is out. Our emotions can become like an out of control locomotive due to the complexities of the fire. People are so fragile . . . . . . .aren't we though?

Here are some situations that can cause extreme complications within. We call them fire burners.

FIRE BURNERS THAT CAN WREAK HAVOC.

[A] The "for sure" business deal that you financially entered into has now gone sour. Not only that, you are deeply in debt and currently see no way out. Additionally, you are being bombarded by creditors demanding repayment of business loans.

[B] Your marriage has taken a serious fall. You hardly communicate intelligently with your spouse. You may even be thinking of separation or divorce. The mental anguish is killing you to the point that you want out no matter the cost to your bank account.

[C] Your teenage child is on drugs in a bad way. You also know that he/she is currently living a very permissive lifestyle. Worse yet is the constant feeling of hopelessness that sets in as parental one-on-one talks and/or outside psychological counseling with your baby seem to fall on deaf ears. You do not know how to cope. All of this causes many sleepless nights which is taking a toll of your health including your psyche.

[D] You've been the victim of corporate downsizing wherein the well-paying job that you cherished is out the window. You have been searching the various employment sections of the web, including hard copies, for six months with no success. Every resume you submit seems to fall into a black hole while your precious savings are evaporating. Thoughts enter your mind such as: I'm over the hill professionally? Am I too old or is my education lacking relative to today's highly competitive market? Is this non-employment issue getting to get to the point where I lose my home and property due to a lack of steady income?

[E] I'm in a [personal] chemistry battle with my employer who does not respect me, my work or my position. As a result promotions have passed by me consecutively. My pay grade is beneath my worth and I've not received a merit increase in over two years. I've attempted for months to find a new job with no success. Maybe I don't measure up to other people's expectations. I do not know what to do. I go to work every day steeped in deep depression expecting the other shoe to drop anytime.

All of these situations—and more—can be the cause of Wit's End represented by sleepless nights and irritable days. Why is this happening? The answer is simple and straight forward. That is you, the Christian, are not in control of your situation. You've not learned to *really* turn matters of this nature over to Him.

I had to learn to stop leading with my head and turn key decisions over to Him!

<u>The most important lesson of this reading is learning to allow The Lord to work things out on your behalf when under a Wit's End umbrella. No matter the pain—stay focused on Him.</u> The Alveys have learned to shut-out the complaining and fast on the word with continuous prayer. REMEMBER, THE ONE THING SATAN AND HIS DOGS CANNOT TOLERATE IS PRAISE TO OUR LORD. WHEN YOU PRAISE OUR LORD YOU SHUT OUT ANY DEMON ATTACK. You will do well to remember this!

Complete freedom from all stress is impossible. Paradoxically too much stress, or elongated stress "that is non-manageable," can contribute to disease-caused conditions, brought on by the body's metabolic imbalance. We've already mentioned this. However, I feel it worth repeating this issue. This situation can subsequently lead towards premature death. It's how you handle Wit's End that matters. What kind of inner response do you possess during the combative situations associated with your stress wars?

> *"Then said I, wisdom is better than strength: nevertheless the poor man's wisdom is despised, and his words are not heard."*
> Ecclesiastes 9:16 KJ

We were stunned to find that 90% of visiting patients to health clinics and hospitals were admitted due to stress and its affiliated symptoms.

Imagine how many of these individuals could have avoided turning themselves over to a health care professional or medical physician if they could have controlled their Wit's End situation through Our Lord? We have great compassion for those fighting uncontrolled situations

Those with various degrees of Wit's End complications represent billions of dollars in lost employment man-hours which equates to about 60% of America's work force calling in sick at one time or another during the yearly work calendar.

ARE YOU CURRENTLY CARRYING A "WIT'S END" SITUATION?

1. If so what is your attitude?
2. How are you handling your situation?
3. Do you strive on stress due to your job [or situation] and therefore

you're able to cope without crashing? Or.
4. Does your battle have you pinned down to the point of continued exhaustion?

EAT RIGHT AND EXERCISE

Speaking of exhaustion. It is important, when you're in the middle of a stress war to eat right. We're not speaking of expensive foods. There are, even with today's (inexcusable) high food, gasoline and home heating oil costs, foods that are somewhat inexpensive and yet highly nutritious.

If you want to know more about our experiences in this area [How we did it] feel free to email me via drfranklinaalvey@aol.com. Our recommendations are not fancy. They are wholesome! What we did kept us in perfect health while on a stiffening budget.

Another area that we recommend [if possible] is the continued state of taking nutriments on top of a balanced diet. You must keep in mind that stress, caused by Wit's End, is a physical detriment or toll on the body. These situations or mental wars are heavily draining on your entire being.

We leave the balance of this issue to your opinion with the exception of one factor. Do you utmost to stay healthy during any stressful situation.
We cannot over emphasize the importance in doing your best in maintaining a proper diet. Respect yourself . . . . just get it done!

If you have the physical capacities consider exercising on a regular basis. Exercise is extremely beneficial for weight reduction and cardiovascular health. It is also a great asset to maintaining stress management and sleep deprivation. You do not need the benefit of an expensive athletic club to maintain a good exercise regimen. One of the greatest exercises is walking which is free. It's a great time to ponder in your mind so as to work out the details or moves relative to your current stressful situation. KEEP BUSY! If you can't get out, during winter months, consider exercise classes as shown on the web. It is also a prudent idea to consider consulting a physician before you attempt a strenuous workout condition three to five days a week. One of the most Spirit Filled nutritional/exercise professionals in the USA in my good friend Coach Don Nava who created and operates the international Totally Fit Life Program which is Christ faith based. You can update your exercise and nutritional program—at no charge—through his best selling web series via www.coach@thetotallyfitlife.com. If you ask he'll put you on his list to receive beneficial health tips.

When you're going through a Wit's End situation do not remain a Lone Ranger. Seek some form of counseling. If you cannot afford a professional counselor, associated with your particular situation, seek out a trusting friend. Counseling is an extremely therapeutic technique used to help you recognize life's priorities and thought processes by identifying the emotional and mental issues. New insights and doors of opportunity can be opened by sharing your situation with those most trusted.

Remember also that when you're "going through" the enemy will have you bring up words of discouragement . . . . words that you will later regret. Again, what is the antidote? Stay in prayer. Always pray.

Alcohol in combination with the vigor's of Wit's End can be deadly. Some feel alcohol promotes a relaxed feeling. The medical world is far more adaptive in explaining the detriments associated with alcohol when connected with Wit's End. Booze and stress create a mental Molotov Cocktail.

We know that alcohol dehydrates the body which induces further stress. We have also known some to remain in an alcohol dream world while simultaneously attempting to ward against their current Wit's End. This is a killer. Now you are walking directly into the fire and you will be severely burned mentally when the fuzz wears off. Stay away from all forms of pornography—on the web—or other alternatives. Don't get involved in "chat rooms" with any sex. Pornography will scar your soul. These conditions will lead you directly to a "Wits End" experience.

LOOKING AT THE BIGGER PICTURE; IT'S NOT GOING TO GET EASIER:

You may find some areas of this report seemingly duplicated or overlapping. This may be so. I am a Watchman and Spiritual Watchmen tend to repeat themselves—at times—making sure everyone hears the word representing the thundering hoof-beats of the impending enemy.

THE APOCALYPSE:

LET'S REMOVE OURSELVES FROM THE IMMEDIATE
PICTURE AND KEY ON THE WORLD SITUATION
THIS IS REPRESENTD BY A TICKING TIME BOMB.

> *"For thus saith The Lord, thy bruise is incurable and thy wound is Grievous."*
>
> *Jeremiah 30:12 KJV*

Michael J. Easley, of the Moody Bible Institute, wrote in his recent letter that America is witnessing a growing secularism that is sweeping the culture within our public schools. An entire generation is being raised to accept immorality and materialism. At the same time, moral relativism has made huge inroads into our culture. Add to this is the widespread, rapid drop in biblical knowledge, and you have perhaps the most serious threat ever facing our nation. The Bible informs us repeatedly what happens to His people when they neglect His law and turn to gods of Baalim.

THINK OF THIS. EVERY COUNTRY, IN THE HISTORY OF MANKIND, FAILED WHEN DISAVOWING GOD AND HIS MANDATES FOR SUCCESS.

Churchill recognized two important things: *"You cannot compromise with evil. Compromise is defeat. The course which follows compromise goes steadily downwards, and unless that compromise is dealt with, decline and decay are inevitable."*

America is facing a cornucopia of complications because of the moral cancer that slowly eats its way into the very heart of our country. Never in the history of America have we faced such inclimate weather patterns which even now are of Biblical proportions. The mental health of our nation is in a catatonic state of negativism due to the economic disasters

caused by a myriad of circumstances of which we are all aware. None of these conditions are happenstance. Stay saved Franklin . . . stay saved!
Christians all over the world have a sense we're living in the final days.

USA TODAY reported that effective June 1, 2008 the State of California officially endorse gay marriages. Since then the endorsement has been overturned. California houses about 2,600,000 Gays.

The number of out of wedlock births in the US jumped by more than a percentage point last year—to 38.5 percent. The US Census Bureau reported. If the current trend continues, in 12 years, half of all US babies will be born to a single mother. Unless I am missing my mark these statistics are not representative of marriage between one man and one woman.

Is God more than displeased with His people? Yes, He is most upset. This is why we can see the commencement of the end taking place.

Since January 22, 1973 [the year abortions became legal] 3,700 unborn babies are executed daily by abortion as reported by The Center for Bio EthicalReform.[http//www.abortionno.org/Resources/fastfacts.html] Some of these doctors and nurses, committing abortions, work on weekends defending whales, mink, otter and other endangered animals. Am I missing something?

> *"The Lord has opened His armory and has brought fourth the weapons of his indignation; behold I am against thee O thou most proud; for the day is come, the time that I will visit thee."*
>
> Jeremiah 50: 25A & 31

Also, log onto: http//thisistheendoftheworldasweknowit.com which also outlines the world plagues that are growing at an alarming rate. In some cases, throughout our world, uncontrolled disease is running rampant.

One of Satan's blindfolds is to keep the people of America [including Christians] busy beyond comprehension. While we have access to all international news channels, including the web and hard copy, we still do not truly discern or fathom the horrid number of trials worldwide, which currently place millions at Wit's End.

Most Americans are up to their necks in work schedules, family, finances, hobbies and the like to really understand yet comprehend the world calamities that are commencing to surround us due to their individual cares and ambitions. Millions of American families are having a difficult time in keeping expenses up due to the cost of oil which impedes all services. As we wrote earlier too many Christians have their ears plugged. That is, their mind only focuses on their individual life. Viz., my family, my trials, my finances, my work schedule, my hobbies, my time to relax, to the point that God's communications cannot get through a plugged ear. Our Lord is pleased to warn us of impending dangers if we will but listen to Him 24/7 through daily continued prayer and Bible study.

His warning is mapped out for this country as outlined in Deuteronomy 8:19 and 20. And He said:

"And it shall be, if thou do at all forget The Lord and walk after other God's and serve them, and worship them, I testify against you this day that you shall surely perish. (20) As the nations which the Lord destroyed before your face, so shall you perish; because you would not be obedient to the voice of The Lord your God."

Again I say that we had better be on the lookout. There are impending signs on the horizon that spell disaster for millions. Here is a good example. The Voice of the Martyrs International recently announced the following. *"54 restricted and hostile nations refuse to allow the Gospel of Chris into their respective lands. This represents 600 million people void of receiving the Bible."* Can you imagine what Our Lord will do to those leaders responsible for refusing His word to be released to their countrymen? Lord have mercy!

ARE YOU UP TO SPEED?

The hot topic, for America right now, is associated with the increased cost of fuel [oil] which indulges itself—in some form or fashion—with practically every consumer product known to our households. I will come back to this later.

Are you wondering where food prices are going? Do you realize what is currently behind these increases? Do you care? You will futuristically! Here are some unfolding issues for your consideration relative to current food challenges combined with today's natural disasters associated with those to come.

A. Because of the scarcity of wheat production Beijing is buying up farmland in Africa and South America. They know, since rice and noodles are a key staple to the Chinese diet, the outlook for future food production is grim. Do you see this as a sign of anything?

B. Continued drought in Australia is causing serious wheat decline. This is not a new issue with the "Down Under people

C. There is a global population explosion in process. By 2050 [just 39 years from now] current meat [beef] consumption will double meaning that it will take 6 more pounds of "livestock feed" to produce one pound of meat. Remember, cloven hoof creatures are herbivores. Concerning "livestock feed." AOL, in a recent report, detailed that it takes 510 pounds of corn to make 13 gallons of ethanol. This corn could be put to better use. [The ethanol thing is far from being over.]

D. Coupled with this is the soaring cost of natural gas which is the main ingredient for production of synthetic fertilizer. This may not seem a big deal until the educational door is opened explaining that 40% of the world's calories are produced with synthetic nitrogenous fertilizers. The cost of natural gas, used to produce fertilizer, is zooming at an unprecedented rate. If it's expensive now where do you think it will in 2018 or just 7 years from now? Do you think the cost of food is expensive today?

E. Increased wheat production means substantially boosting our grain output which simply requires far more farmland. The paradox, at least in the US, is that farmland is shrinking due to the construction of new shopping centers, golf courses and the like. Yes America still has an abundant of barren land available for crop production. Unfortunately to much if it is arid and void of water.

F. By 2055 the world's population will increase by 4 billion. Will we have enough land to produce the required food needs?

G. It is extremely expensive to produce natural gas which is required for the sake of fertilizer production; we'll also need a trillion extra tons of water—to meet wheat growing demands—from a planet already seriously overdrawn on its water accounts. It is predicted that nations—as well as our US Government including individual US land owners—will ride shotgun over their water supplies. Water will be an extremely—gun toting issue—hot issue. It is already in many areas.

H. The current "Extreme Jump in Weather Events" could seriously hamper world grain powerhouses like the USA and Europe. Linked to this is the nation of Africa where current food production has suffered for years. World wheat production for 2008-09 was predicted at 656,013 metric tons compared to 606,400 actual metric tons in 2007-08. This is only a 9.2% predicted increase. Our world population in 2007 was six billion, six hundred seventy seven million. 2008 has brought to six billion, seven hundred fifty five million. I am asking you again; do you see the emerging picture regarding the world's food production? Food production is the number one challenge worldwide. Our Lord could use food production complications, along with natural disasters, to wake His people up. It would not be the first time.

1. Connected to all of this is world weather. The national Weather Service is predicting that 2011 will represent the deadliest tornado season in decades while the National Oceanic and Atmospheric Administration (www.NOAA.com) predicted a much higher tornado season in 2011. They now agree this to be a gross understatement. Do you again see the embryonic of a deadly picture forming here? Yes we've had nasty tornado/hurricane seasons

of past. But when you combine them with the uncontrolled world floods, cyclones, massive nation crippling earthquakes, continued and numerous out of control fires in the US, the rumors of so many impending wars—all in simultaneousness—the picture emerging is one that grows larger. A monster that cannot be controlled. It will get to the point that no nation, no matter the bank roll or number of National Guard troops, will be able to keep these drastic conditions in check.

AOL provided the following report May 29, 2008. "Under a court order and four years late, the White House produced what it called a science-based 'one-stop shop' of specific threats to the United States from man-made global warming. The report was required by a 1990 law which says that every four years the government must produce a comprehensive science assessment of global warming. This report has not been produced since 2000. Environmental groups produced a court order *[in 2010]* to force the Bush administration to publicly display the document by the end of May." [Italics Alvey]

SOON YOU'LL SEE A LOT MORE OF THIS ON CABLE NEWS

1. Increased heat heaths deaths from climate-worsened smog, in Los Angeles alone, in yearly fatalities, could increase by more than 1,000 by 2080, and the Midwest and Northeast are most vulnerable to increased heat deaths.

2. Worsening water shortages for agriculture and urban users. From California to New York, lack of water will be an issue.

3. A need for billions of dollars in more power plants (one major cause of global warming gases) to cool a hotter country. A summer cooling will mean Seattle's energy consumption would increase by 146 percent with the warming that could come by the end of this century.

4. More deaths and damage from wildfires, hurricanes and other natural disasters and extreme weather. In the last three decades, wildfire season in the West has increased by 78 days.

5. Increased insect infestations and food and water borne microbes and diseases. [Current] Insect and pathogen outbreaks to the forest are causing $1.5 billion in losses. [Italics added]

6. Climate change is very likely to accentuate the disparities already evident in the American health care system. Many of the expected health effects are likely to fall disproportionately in the poor, the elderly, the disabled and the uninsured.

7. In 2008, 15.6 million American's could not pay their utility bills. This is represented by 5 billions owed to the utility companies. These bills are owed from that previous winter. What happens to these tax payers come the fall of 2011 if they're unable to catch up? Do they burn their furniture? The situation has become worse since 2010.

8. We all know our economy is in trouble; the credit market is a

mess; residential home values are destroyed; commodity prices are up and unemployment is up. Added to this is the unparalleled cost of auto/truck fuel; Consumer Reports magazine advised that 80% of Americans aren't planning the purchase a new vehicle in the next year. GM's and Chrysler bond had dropped to B—minus or six levels below investment grade while some Chrysler loans had traded at 50 cents on the dollar backing up the possibility of bankruptcy. Through all of this the Stock Market advised that, during this century, they had never seen such devastating losses since the great depression. God is shaking everything up! Do you see these are great warning signs building?

9. Forty percent of the homes available for sale in California's Orange County are either in foreclosure or priced below the value of the current owner's mortgage.

10. Government regulators seized Pasadena's Indy Mac BankCorp, with assets of over $19 billion representing one of the Nation's largest bank failures. Indy Mac has 7,200 employees.

11. Fannie May and Freddy Mac, responsible for over 6 trillion on loans and mortgages, are near closure due to the write off of so many billions in bad loans

Some people say, "That's OK. I won't be here when most of this stuff comes down. Or, I won't fall that low financially!" Really! You do not know. Second, what about those of you who have children? They'll be here. Bring them up in the admonition of the The Lord and He will see that they are cared for under protection of His leadership.

Back to the subject of food production. The Oregonian [May 25, 2008] in its OPINION section produced the following:

> "Meanwhile, around the world, food prices have almost doubled in three years, Asian rice prices have nearly tripled in one year, and food riots have exploded across much of the globe. The United Nations Food and Agriculture Organization issued a report that the worst price hikes might be complete but the overall food prices would stay high . . . . the number of hungry will increase by many more millions of people.

Do you think Our Lord is upset relative to the reading of Michael Easley's [Moody Bible] comments combined with the number of aborted babies along with the other facts provided by the international world news agencies? If you agree then you'll witness increased tension, within our nation, which will make the term Wit's End, with increased numbers of individuals and families, as common as Smith or Jones.

Today we hop to the store and pick up what we need in a jiffy. I am predicting that within our time frame [10 to 15 years] the ease of shopping, as we know it today, will change in a way that will make it substantially more difficult. This is why we hope you will learn the lessons of coping now versus being caught up without warning.

If you really think world conditions are going to improve or oil prices will drop to reasonableness, save minor periodical adjustments, then you had better return to your physician asking for a refund on your last lobotomy. The recent attack on India's top people attraction is just one more sign.

Many young people just out of college, who are commencing their business careers, have the opinion that someday they'll be able to retire with that second home just as their parents and forefathers did. I am prophesying that the American's of this age, attempting retirement between 2038 and 2045, will never see that phase of luxury. The Lord will never allow this nation that kind of futuristic prosperity due to the apostasy taking place in our country today. I need not display additional sordid details outlining the demise of our nation. We all know what's happening.

Irrespective, some may say that Alvey needs to have his mind renewed or the metal plate in his head is coming loose. I believe that my statement holds truth. Look at the warning signs posted for our benefit

> *"And it shall be, if thou do at all forget the Lord and walk after other god's and serve them, and worship them, I testify against you this day that you shall surely perish. (20) As the nations which the Lord destroyed before your face, so shall you perish; because you would not be obedient to the voice of the Lord your God.*
>
> *Deuteronomy 8: 19-20 KJV*

Lord Have Mercy!

THAT'S THE DILEMA. WHAT IS THE GOOD NEWS?

And He said: *"I will both lay me down in PEACE, and sleep, for thou Lord, only makes me dwell in safety."*
Psalms 4:8 KJV

And He said: *"Thou will keep him in perfect peace, whose mind is stayed on thee: because he trusts in thee."*
Isaiah 26:3 KJV

And He said: *"Peace I leave with you, my peace I give to you: not as the world gives [I give you perfect peace] Let not your heart be troubled, neither let it be afraid."*
John 14:27 KJV [Brackets AlveyI]

There is a need for a spiritual cellar, a deep under-ground cavern, capable of holding you and your loved ones during the oncoming storm. This needs to be place of protection that will keep you safe during the most desperate of times. Note we used the term SPIRITUAL CELLAR.

I am once more reminded of Professor Alfred Edersheim who so eloquently describes the ability of doing God's will during horrific periods. He writes:

"Scripture-History is full of seemingly strange contrasts. Unintelligible to the superficial observer, [however] the believing heart rejoices to trace in them, side by side, the difference between what appears to the eye of man and what really is before God. If once we enter on such a course, it will probably not be long before we cast to the wind any scruples about the means to be employed. Here faith is the only true remedy: faith which leaves God to carry out His own purposes, content to trust Him absolutely, and to follow Him whithersoever HE leadeth, And God's way is never through the thicket of human cunning and devices. 'He that believeth shall not make haste,' nor need he, for God will do it all for him." IBID [Italics mine]

Most Christians believe that Our Lord Jesus will forgive them of their sins; they believe the Bible is the spoken word of God; they will testify of His goodness; they will dance in His Church aisles and wave Christian flags. Yet, the majority of these good folks do not believe that this same Christ will pull them through a hard place. Most individuals, under this covering, will never confess aloud of their disbelief. The number of God's people fitting this description is innumerable. *"Ah, lord God! Behold, thou has made the heaven and the earth by thy great power and stretched out arm, and there is nothing to hard for thee."* *[Jeremiah 32:17 [KJV].* If our people could only [TRULY] believe and trust God for his many blessings there would be untold benefits coming to them which they now go without because of unbelief and ignorance of His will. If nothing is too hard for Him, and He has promised us all our needs and lawful wants, here and hereafter, then there is no excuse for lack of faith.

Some people have been saved 30 years or more. After this elongated period they know no more about Jesus Christ today than the day they were saved. They attend Church on a regular basis. Their only reason for attending services is the ability [feel good] to jump and shout with the choir. Once they have their "Spiritual Fix" they shuffle off to take up where they commenced pre-Church day. This leads to nowhere. They fail to understand the verisimilitude of Christ.

Paradoxically, the secular world seems to have more faith in completing projects accomplished, through their own efforts, than Christians who attempt to secure accomplished tasks through Christ.

Here is a list of individual—secular—people who believed in succeeding no matter how many times they were turned away:

1. J.K Rowling's book, "Harry Potter and the Philosopher's Stone", was rejected 12 times before a small London publisher picked it up.
2. Decca Records turned down a contract with the Beatles saying, "we don't like their sound."
3. Walt Disney was fired by a newspaper editor who said he lacked imagination.
4. Michael Jordan was cut from his high-school varsity basketball team.

5. Steve Jobs was rebuffed by Atari, Inc. and Hewlett Packard when he and his partner attempted to sell the Apple Computer system.
6. Dr. Seuss made one more attempt to secure a publisher after his 27th rejection.

The list is endless representing secular individuals seeking fame and fortune. They simply did not give up. Jesus Christ is the world's greatest publisher, business consultant, lobbyist, inventor, educator, creator, physician and parent. If we believed in Him to help us achieve our projects and accomplishments, as much as these six people believed in their own talents, the world book publishers would not be capable of house the number of miracles produced.

> And He said: "for the children of this world are in their generation wiser than the children of light."
>
> Luke 16:8b KJV

Yes there are dark troubling days ahead for this nation as well as the entire world. How many times a day do you witness, on CNN or FOX, the devastation taking place in our country due to the escalating cost of fuel which immediately ricochets from the gas pump to the grocery store food shelf? As of December 2008 auto fuel has dropped from $4 plus to under $2. Don't fool yourself. Fuel prices will not remain there! As of this writing gasoline prices hover around $3.75 to $4.50 for regular gas. This and other drastic situations are not reasons for us to walk in fear, trepidation, or apprehension. On the contrary, Our Lord apprised us to look at the good things through His word.

"These things I have spoken unto you, that in me you might have peace. In the world you shall have tribulation: But be of good cheer; I have overcome the world."

John 16:33 KJV

If Barbara and I have learned one thing during our trials it is this. He said to us many times, "I did not say your situation would be easy. I said that would take care of you in the midst of your trials as long as you kept me in your heart." He has never failed once to make sure we were kept even in the absolute darkest days of our dilemma.

The Price of Inaction Is Far Greater Than The Cost of a Mistake.
The Economist

Ever since our teaching trails commenced we've had goals that were Christ oriented.

Nothing glam, rather, we have found following Him at all costs will create an everlasting reserve parachute in time of need. What sort of goals do we mean? First, we never involved ourselves with the secular faith business of "Blab it and grab it." Nor did we seek out the positive thinking business that motivational companies make millions off of.

It grieves me when so many people will pay $250.00 for a series of CD's including an educational binder full of clever clichés depicting stories of "Winners" who made it in spite of mind bending obstacles? The information within these packages is usually pretty accurate as long as you have a job as an anchor or a revenue stream to attach yourself to.

How effective are these zesty catches and winning business personalities, along with their harmonizing stories, when: (1) you lose your job, (2) your child dies, (3) your home is devastated by floods, (4) your spouse contracts cancer which is then connected with great pain and financial loss, (5) fire destroys your home or (6) A financial disaster pulls you into bankruptcy destroying your lives therefore making you a credit leper?

When Wit's End enters your life you pull your spiritual reserve parachute calling on Our Lord to cover you with His blessing and protection. Campy motivational seminars will not provide a covering of this magnitude. This is when being a goal orientated Christian pays off. Only Christ removes hurts that totally crush the individual's soul. If you have goals—through Christ—you're ready for war!

If you are not a Christian this portion of reading may not make sense as so many non-faith people believe running secular statements repeatedly through your mind will clear up overwhelming challenges. If this were true the Bible would still not be the number one best selling book worldwide.

WHAT DO WE MEAN BY CHRIST CENTERED GOALS?

> "And Jesus said unto them, come after me and I will make you to become fishers of men. And straightaway they forsook their nets and followed Him."
> Mark 1:17-18 KJV

In order to follow Him they had to have goals. Since the New Testament had not been written He was their goal. That is why He spent about three years teaching them how to become goal centered. It is central to say that after He left earth they followed the goals He had left them.

Today Christians have two significant factors available as anchors enabling us to set and follow goals. They are: (1) The Holy Ghost as unction or guide and (2) the Bible as a physical teaching and instructional tool. If you are truly walking with Him these are the only two tools you will ever need to stay in line with your goals. Yes, there are outside written helpers. Irrespective, these two are your spiritual heart and neurological systems.

STEPS TO SUCCESS IN GOAL ACCOMPLISHMENT

1. Decide where you are now with Our Lord.

    What is your relationship with Our Lord at present? Are you and He on the same page? Is there any sin in your life that is keeping you from acquiring favor with Him? Make sure you and He are waking together before attempting any goal setting.

2. Decide what you really need as a goal.

Be realistic. Our Lord is not going to provide you with a position as NY City Firefighter in two years if you're now only 14 years old. Our Lord will not violate man's rule in order to establish our wish.

3. Decide why you desire this goal.

Our Lord has no objection if your desire is to own a Cadillac. His only objection comes when the car becomes a god to the owner. Make sure your goal is capable of standing behind Our Lord versus He having to take second place.

4. Decide why you want/need this goal.

You may be unemployed and therefore need a new job or there may be sickness within your family and therefore the gift of healing is the goal. It is important to remember that Jesus will care for you [your family] while your goal is being sought as long as you and He is walking together.

DO NOT BECOME DISCOURAGED if your goal is not met within YOUR TIME schedule. If discouragements sets in seek out counseling through your Pastor or locate a friend to confide in. Do not be a Lone Ranger. If you attempt to stand alone the enemy may crush you.

5. Constantly picture the goal in your mind.

Picture that new home, representing your goal, in your mind. Think of it constantly. Thank The Lord for the goal which is coming. Acquire scriptures that are associated with your goal.

Memorize these scriptures. Talk to the enemy "aloud" each time a discouraged thought comes into your mind. Continuously praise Our Lord EVEN IF YOU DO NOT FEEL LIKE IT. Put pictures of your goal on the wall and look at them. *During the early period of 1980 we were so poor that at times it became impossible to buy a $3.00 magazine. We put pictures of new Mercedes Benz on our walls. In 1988 we purchased our new 420SL Mercedes Benz.*

6. **Decide on a plan of action once you obtain your goal.**

(1) When your goal comes in be sure and thank Our Lord. Praise Him for His goodness for protecting you during the period of waiting.

(2) Immediately set up additional or new goals. Realize that He has and wants to bless you. Our Lord desires to bring you all of your needs and wants. The only reason Christians lose out here is (A) they won't stay saved, (B) They will not wait for Him to move on their behalf

. . . They launch out on their own which is deadly!

"Vision belongs to all who are willing to commit their lives to their goals. After commitment, the decisions are simple because vision is that quality enabling and empowering us to pay the price."

Charlie "Tremendous" Jones

Seven reasons why Christians do not have goals.

1. They do not know what they want.

2. They do not believe that Our Lord will provide.

3. They do not understand the difference between setting God oriented goals and wishing.

4. They confuse working with God versus working toward the goal while leaving Him out.

5. They do not understand true "Setting Goal Standards" with Our Lord.

6. They act (now) urgently versus waiting on God to move on their

behalf. Moving out on your own may lead you to quicksand.

7. Serving Christ without goals is like throwing your fishing line in the water with no bait. Fisherpersons who attempt to catch their dinner using this method do so my hoping that "something" eatable will accidently snag itself on the hook. This method throws God's word to the wind or banking that you're [needed] blessing will come through good luck. Barbara and I do not know anything about luck. We do not bank on it and we are afraid of people who do. Opportunity through Our Christ is the only true measure that brings qualified opportunity representing quality of blessing backed by His peace.

REMEMBER!

In your goal setting remember to: [A] Write them out; [B] Make them personal between you and The Lord; [C] Continually thank The Lord for bringing you the goal that you cannot yet see; (Hebrews 11:1)
[D] Be sure your goal is encompassing, be specific; [E] Make sure your goal is compatible with the word; [F] Be absolutely sure that your goal is realistic; [G] That your goal is workable. Viz., Not asking to become an astronaut when you still lack a high school education.

We could have written extensive chapters on goal setting. This is not our intention. What you read here are the basic procedures that the Alveys have used very successfully for years, there are many Christian goal setting books on this subject throughout a myriad of sources. We would suggest seeking alternative Christian education on goal setting if you desire. Our only warning is please be careful what you read. Instead: read, fast, pray, obey! Following these four words will cause Him to reveal his will for you. Many people put on a Christian face just to sell their books and tapes thus leading Saints down the wrong path.

OUR FINAL WORD ON GOAL SETTING.

1. Set a goal for your life that demands your best efforts.

2. Develop a burning desire to do the best—a passion to win!

3. Keep your eye on the goal set before you at all times. This can be accomplished through prayer and scripture memorization. Constantly think goals.

4. Stay close to people who will encourage. Do not mix with those who are negative. Refuse to be critical. Remain aloof from negative spirits. Do not mix with people who will pull you down.

5. Look for a personal lesson out of every situation. This is how God speaks to you while the goal is in transit. These are also training lessons. EXPECT TRIALS DURING THE WAITING PERIOD. Understand why!!!

6. Be a light for Jesus where you are. This is part of reaching goals as it helps to keep you positive.

7. Practice self control of your emotions. Lay aside critical situations. Don't strike back just

because you're having a bad hair day.

8. BELIEVE, THROUGH OUR LORD, THAT YOUR GOAL WILL BE REACHED WITH SUCCESS.

9. Jesus Christ is the world's most persistent person. I know this because He never gave up on me no matter what I was going through. *Barbara and I had some days where we wept together uncontrollably. However, we refused to give up even though at times the next day was worse than the day before.*

10. Lord, what are your goals for me while I am setting goals through you?

11. Remember, you will never outgrow warfare. You must learn to fight using the Holy Spirit as your shield. If it will work for the Alveys it will create success for all Christians.

12. Failure is not the end. It's just an opinion of Satan. Push on!

13. You must allow failure into your life. It cannot happen without your permission.

14. Struggling to reach your goals is living proof that you have not been and will not be conquered by the enemy.

    Be bold as the friend of God—importune—urge with frequent solidification

    . . . be tenacious in purpose stubbornly adhering to a purpose; continue steadily, incessant. Refuse to give an inch, be desperate, demanding, insistent, eager

and troublesome in pursuit of His promises. "Lord you promised me!"

I have learned that pain is simply Satan's weakness leaving my body.

15. There is no way, under the sun, that Saints attain their goals logically. Just obey His voice and go forward.

16. The darkest days are always just before dawn and warfare always surrounds the birth of a miracle.

17. No one has ever been a loser longer than Satan.

18. EVERY DAY —CONTINUALLY —THANK OUR LORD FOR GRANTING YOUR GOALS. REPEAT YOUR REQUEST

IRRESPECTIVE THE PRESSURE YOU'RE UNDER.

And He said, *"Wherefore criest unto me, speak...."*

Exodus 14:15

ARE WE WINNING EVEN THOUGH THE CLOUDS BE DARK?

You've read a substantial amount of data here describing battles created by Satan and totally overcome by God. So, are we as a Christian people actually winning the battle through the war?

"You betcha" [A quote from Governor Sarah Palin]

Here is a perfect example of Christ's Church taking center stage. You may never have heard of E.A. Adeboye, but the Pastor of the Redeemed Christian Church of God is one of the most successful preachers in the world. He broadcasts that his Church has outposts in 110 countries. He has 14,000 branches—claiming 5 million members—in his home country of Nigeria alone. There are 360 RCCG Churches in Britain, and about the same number in U.S. cities like Chicago, Dallas, and Tallahassee, Florida. This man of God has sent missionaries to China and such Islamic countries as Pakistan and Malaysia. He desires to save souls and he'll do this by planting Churches the same way Starbucks used to builds coffee shops: everywhere.

He informed NEWSWEEK that his goal is to have Churches within five minutes' walk of every person.

Adeboye is, as you guessed it, a Pentecostal preacher and a man of God's miracles, and Pentecostalism is [as you know] the biggest, fastest growing Christian movement since the Reformation.

GOVERNOR PALIN IS NOT ASHAMED OF THE GOSPEL

One of the strangest images from the 2008 campaign was the You Tube clip of Alaska Gov. Sarah Palin in church, head bowed, palms turned up toward heaven, standing silently as Thomas Muthee, a Pentecostal Preacher from Kenya, prayed for her. The clip (and NEWSWEEK) triggered its own little culture skirmish, with secular observers calling Palin "a wack job" and conservative Christians responding "There's nothing wrong with her Church!!!"

Few commentators on either side noted how normal Palin's scene was to hundreds of millions of Christians around the globe.

YES WE ARE WINNING!

The world now has about 600 million Pentecostals, the largest group of Christians after the Roman Catholics. In Asia, the number of Pentecostals has grown from about 10 million to 166 million since 1970, according to the study for the Center for The study of Global Christianity at Gordon-Conwell Theological Seminary. In Latin America, Pentecostals have expanded from 13 million to 151 million; in North America, from 19 million to 77 million; and in Africa, from 18 million to 156 million. By 2050 most of Africa will be Christian, estimates Grant Wacker, professor of Christian history at Duke University and most of those Christians will be Pentecostals.

At this point I urge you to read <u>C.T. STUDD Cricketer & Pioneer</u> by Norman Grubb. You see, Studd was the first Christian Missionary to penetrate the deep part of Africa commencing in 1906 and from page 119 of his book are these words: "He (God) said that in the middle of the continent there were numbers of tribes who had never heard of the story of Jesus Christ. He (was) told that explorers had been to those regions, and big game hunters, Arabs, and traders, European officials and scientist, but no Christians had ever gone to tell of Jesus . . . . I said why have no Christians gone? God replies, 'why don't you go?'"

Little did Studd realize—now over 100 years later—that the Christian seeds he planted then would produce a Christian nation by the middle of the 21st Century. Yes we are winning!

REFLECTIONS

If I, as an outsider, were to read this book I might think twice before considering becoming a Christian. Some of the hardships described herein are overwhelming and I do not know if I would even consider

Christ seeing all the "stuff" I might have to endure.

There are distinctions to keep in mind. First, the Bible clearly states that some are chosen (John 15:16) by Him for a particular mission. In many of these cases these individuals—when selected by Christ—might have to endure horrific trials in order to mold them so as to meet the requirements and designated use as Christ's representatives. Any judgment or trial which does not break the [human] nature and subdues one's life—for His glory—only hardens it for tomorrow's battle. As the sun hardens river clay, rain also softens the same so it can be molded again.

A good case in point revolves around the Disciples including especially St. Paul. The Alveys were one family chosen specifically to represent Him through the gift of helps.

Notice the word gift? In order to attain this spiritual vocation a lot of changes must [had to] take place in order to remove the world given consisting of any pride or vanity. The lives of Barbara and Franklin have been strategically altered through our trials. We now know, at 71 and 78 respectfully, that Our Lord put us through every trial in order for us to learn the background behind "Don't Waste Your Sorrow." What He meant for us was a training ground designated to remove our eyes from self and place them on Him. Only when this is accomplished can we thoughtfully think of others first versus falling into the traditional trap of "What about Me?"

THE CALLING

Franklin, as a teen, through the military and college was a very emotionally resilient individual. I was raised by strong parents whose motto was simply "get it done."

While in college I was voted one of the 10 most popular men on the Oregon State University campus. After college I took my interviews ending up in a small Fortune 500 Company. I was the second highest award winner in the company and within four years became Assistant Vice-President charged with overseeing a $25 million dollar division. That was big money in 1966. From there I just kept climbing with Barbara and the kids, in tow, right behind me. Companies, knowing of your ability to make corporate profits, will use you to the fullest extent. This may mean corporate transfers into areas that need help. During my career my company transferred me—along with Barbara and the kids from our first home in Scottsdale, Arizona—to Prince George B.C. Canada, Tulsa, Oklahoma, St. Louis, Missouri, Boston, Massachusetts, Iowa City, Iowa, Edmonton, Alberta Canada, Vancouver B.C., Canada, Spokane, Washington and finally Bellevue, Washington. Some of these years were wonderful, financially rewarding and exciting. My company also sent me corporately to rescue missions in Caracas, Venezuela, Panama City, Panama, Seoul, Korea, Mexico City, Mexico and Tokyo, Japan.

SOME UNBELIEVABLE MIND BLOWING MIRACLES THAT ONLY GOD COULD PRODUCE.

THE RED STRING

I write of this incident as it shows how Our Lord will protect those who, while meaning well, are still outside His will.

My mission, while visiting Tokyo, was to shore up more of an effective relationship with that office as we desired to substantially increase our profit margins. Our Japanese representative met me at the Tokyo

International Airport where he ushered me to the Hilton Hotel. His advice was to get some rest as I was to be a guest that night at his private club.

That night we entered this very posh and fashionable restaurant and were immediately ushered to a private booth. I had just—innocently—picked up the restaurant's menu when two very young attractive ladies slid besides me and my Japanese representative. I thought, "Something is very wrong here." I came to discuss company business and I did not appreciate this interruption. Then the women sitting next to me slid her hand onto my thigh and begin to rub. I immediately commenced to pray that Our Lord would somehow get me out of this mess as it finally dawned upon me that I was in the middle of a high class brothel and I was expected to sleep with this call girl tonight.

I could not very well stand up and yell," HEATHON DOGS . . . BE AWAY FROM ME!" My company needed to retain this account. The competition was stiff within our industry including the fact that my company had spent an enormous amount of money to get me to our Far East station. Additionally, in three days I was due to meet our other representatives in Seoul, Korea and if I destroyed this evening the whole trip might turn into a financial disaster. I knew had I had failed this mission; our company president would not have accepted my story of an unsuccessful business venture gone wrong.

Suddenly, the prostitute assigned to me by my host [who thought I would be thrilled] noticed a red piece of yarn tied around my wrist.

The week before I departed Seattle, Barbara and I had attended an evangelistic crusade at our Church. The evangelist had asked for volunteers who wished blessings from Our Lord through answered prayers. Barbara and I immediately stepped forward—among the hundreds of others—with the same wish. Each person was given an anointed piece of red string. We were told to tie the red band around our wrist thanking Jesus for His answer to our prayer every time we noticed our wrist object. We were instructed never to remove our string, by our Christ centered crusader, with the instructions that when the yarn fell off your prayer request had been answered through His anointing.

My assigned girl asked the meaning of this unusual red object? I explained that Christ was the center of my life and that this red object was a simple reminder to me as to who was in charge of my daily activities. She yelled, "YOU CHRISTIAN? ME CHRISTIAN TOO!

Our Lord had broken the ice. We discussed Church in general for the balance of the evening. I diplomatically, was attempting very delicately not to offend my host, explaining the full meaning of my string. I was capable, by the time we completed our lengthy discussion, to excuse myself due to exhaustion caused by the International time differences including that fact that a full day awaited me tomorrow. I believe my host desired staying however he honored my move. Before departing the restaurant that night, I gave my new found female friend a hug advising that I would pray for her.

My race horse trip across the Far East became a complete success due to a simple red string anointed with the Blood of Christ and to this day Barbara has her string which is used as a Bible book mark.

LOOK IN THE TRUNK!

During one of our periods, represented by the loss of everything including house and car, our Pastor allowed us his second car which enabled us the opportunity to remain mobile.

We had so little money. Barbara and I could make it by living on dry cereal. However, it became a different story with two hungry school age children to feed. At one point we were—as a complete family—setting at our dinner table. The food on our plates was all that was remaining of any substance. We had, other than what food fronted us, a quart of milk, a box of dry cereal and a half loaf of bread in our household. Our total remaining cash totaled $76.15. Any money associated with savings or checking accounts had been drained long ago.

I interject an important point here. We kept nothing from our children relative to our current economic condition. Complete open communication—relating to our trial—was paramount.

We took a family vote concerning our remaining cash. We could (1) shop one more time allowing the family a small amount of food for a short period. Disaster faced us if we ran out of food and we knew it. (2)

The second choice given to vote was in putting the entire amount—$76.15—in the Sunday Church offering which happened to be the same Sunday of our vote. Greg our oldest, said, "Dad, let's put the whole thing in the offering and trust God to see what He will do." The rest of the family agreed.

During our plight none of our fellow Church members knew of our condition save and except our Pastor and we asked him to keep our condition between his office and Our Lord. We needed our Lord's to rescue us and we believed He would. We simply did not know how He would feed us.

When we came out of that same Sunday Church service there was a note attached to the Pastor's car he had allowed us to use, since the bank had reclaimed ours. The note read, "Look in the Trunk!" When we lifted the trunk lid we observed over a dozen bags of groceries dedicated to the Alvey family from loving Church members who knew our plight. This all commenced when a small boy by the name of Greg Alvey believed His Jesus would honor a simple request. His parents followed and the rest is history. What a boy . . . what a God!

I CAN'T REPAY THE $10,000.00

Our company, a research and Development Company responsible for my international business trips, had crashed due to a lack of capital. R&D costs, for high-tech upstart companies is enormously expensive. We were flying high when the State of Washington denied us permission to file for an additional or second $1,000,000.00 intra-state stock offering due to our auditors missing the filing due date. State laws, at that time, required that Washington Corporations wait six months before reapplying after an attempted to file failed. We simply did not have enough capital to remain fluid for such a period.

I held the position as Senior Vice President of Development International. My duties involved the overseeing of stock sales within the State of Washington; making presentations to corporate boards or their senior representatives both national and international who were interested in purchasing our products once R&D completed its tasks including the commencement of production. My traveling and presentation schedule was beyond logic. I was either in the Far East, South America or hoping, through negotiations somewhere in the US, that some American company would consider major investments into our R&D.

I had sold, when the company was solvent, $10,000.00 in stock to the owner of Longview, Washington's largest grocery store. Now the company was dead in the water. All employees were dismissed including this writer. Anyone who had put money into our dream would never see the results.

About two months passed—since closing—when I received a phone call at home from my former Longview client asking how his stock portfolio was doing? I asked if he, as investor, had received our notice. He responded by saying . . . . what notice? I gulped hard and diplomatically explained the fall of our company and that he had lost his $10,000.00 investment. I was ready to say that I can't repay the $10,000.00.

Did he say to me, "you mean to tell me that I lost all . . . . or how am I going to recoup my financial loss . . . . or you swindled me?" No he made no mention of his own feelings. Instead, without a change in voice characterization, he asked how I was doing; was my family suffering due to a loss of income and did we have enough to eat? I explained that things were a bit difficult especially with two young children, who under normal circumstances, ate like growing elephants.

Without further discussion on his part he said, "Franklin, I want you to find the biggest station-wagon or pickup possible and head for my store in Longview. We'll fill up your vehicle with food for your family. When you come into the store ask for me." Then he promptly hung up.

About a week later I drove away from his Longview store with assorted groceries totaling $1,584.00 which lasted our entire family in excess of three months.

About a year and a half later, when the Alvey family became solvent again, I unannounced drove to Longview and saw my friend. In my hand was a check for $1,584.00. I presented my former client with his refund. He took one look at his money and tore the check in half. Then, looking me squarely in the face said, "Franklin, it was God who fed you, not me!"

I left Longview a different man and I have never looked back.

This is just another example of how Our Lord took care of the Alveys all during our financial crash to include our rebuilding program. He knew I always meant well even though my career had come ahead of Our Lord. I was, in some respects, to driven to know any better.

I have never, in my 52 years of marriage, kissed another woman with or through passion as our Lord selected for me the queen of the Oregon State University campus. Our marriage—with trials—has been beautiful. However, I did, as you have read, have a concubine which was my career. This was, as you see, corrected through the breaking trials provided herein by our Lord. He taught me, through tough love that I can only serve one God through

Jesus Christ. Did I learn through my trials? Yes I did thank God!

There is one thing terribly wrong with story. I was saved at age 14 and God had called me as a child to serve him. But I wasn't interested . . . . I had money to make so as to raise my family in a country club atmosphere. For an extended period, through great corporate stress, this worked. We lived in 4,000 square foot homes and belonged to the right associations. I made sure to be politically, economically and socially correct. Years passed, with regular Church service, yet I continued to ignore God's call.

Those of you who know Christ, as a personal savior, are well aware that there is no way—save and except death—one can run from God. He'll pull you down—including the performing of any human act to attract—or get your attention.

In about 1975 my career commenced to slow down. Mr. B.M.O.C. (big man on campus} was literally being shot out of the sky. Everything I touched fell apart including MY beloved finances. I kept asking our Lord for help however my plea always fell on deaf ears. Have I been humbled? Yes, I have been humbled!

Carefully reading Isaiah gives one a clue as to His determination to retain you once He has called you.

> You have trusted in your wickedness and have said, No one sees me
> Your wisdom and knowledge mislead you when you say to yourself,
> I am, and there is none besides me.
> Disaster will come upon you, and you will not know how to conjure it away. A calamity will fall upon you that you cannot ward off with a Ransom;

a catastrophe you cannot foresee will suddenly come upon you.
Isaiah 47:10-11 NIV

The Lord was simply saying, "Franklin, if you will not heed to my call, through gentle nudges, I will place you in a series of trials which I am sure will awake you to my calling." I am sure this book now has more logic to it than at commencement.

As Paul Harvey Used to Say, "Now you've heard The Rest of the Story."

As I look back I am reminded of the infamous quote from Isaiah 48:18

> "O that thou had harkened to my commandments; then had thy peace been as a river and thy righteousness as the waves of the sea."

Therefore, in 1979 I was ordained into the Ministry as Elder. In 2004 I was named Senior Associate Pastor and Chief Operations Officer of Emmanuel Church—Portland, Oregon. This is the position I hold today.

What if I had not heeded to the Lord's call? I'll never know except to say that, in my case, I believe He would have ended my life due to the fact that I possessed a stubborn, reprobate mind. If I stood before Him, at death and He asked me, "Franklin, what did you do for the kingdom of God while on earth?" We all know what that a response would have been.

My trials were—as I look back—a great compliment in that He would select and stay with such a stubborn person as myself.

I have—including my beautiful wife—such wonderful peace. And without His calling I never would have had the capacity—through Him—to help so many broken people including the drunks, those with suicidal minds, broken marriages, the extremely depressed and many more.

A number of years ago I was tempted to reenter the business world—thus leaving the Church as the opportunity of big money again seemed so tempting. Barbara pleaded with me to listen before I made that all important phone call to the company interested in my abilities.

She said, "The responsibility, Our Lord has offered you, to give back to the community is a gift that few have the opportunity to participate in. Others, who receive the call you did, pass up His voice as they're too busy to hear the Holy Ghost. Remember, if you leave you'll be stepping down. If you took the position as CEO of General

Motors with $50 Million in salary and stock options you would still be stepping down. If you leave God will choose someone else to take your place. This means you will miss His blessing including the gift that Jesus has and will provide for you through Emmanuel Church and Bishop C.T."

I am so glad that I listened to Barbara and that through her the Holy Spirit was able to penetrate my thick head. God provided me with three all important situations when I married Barbara. First, he allowed me to marry someone whose IQ far outshines mine. Second, He allowed me to marry a person far better looking than this writer, and third He gave me someone who loved the Lord long before I met her.

STRESS AND MISCOMMUNICATIONS ARE TWO KILLERS THAT DESTROY MOST MARRIAGES. SO HOW DID WE SURVIVE ALL THESE YEARS WHILE FACING SO MANY BACK-TO-BACK TRIALS?

1. <u>Communicate, communicate and communicate:</u> Barbara and always talked things out no matter how difficult the subject was. I can remember we being up all night [9PM—2AM] talking over
Three very painful situations. However, in the end we could hug each other and say with sincerity, "I'm sorry."
2. <u>Be a good sounding board to each other:</u> When you spouse comes to you with a problem they aren't necessarily looking for a solution. Many times they just want you to

listen . . . . they may need to simply get something they deem serious out of their system.
3. <u>*Do not judge:*</u> You desire to be treated with respect. All your spouse ever wants from you is love and one of the real issues of love is giving. How can I give love to my spouse if I, in simultaneousness, judge?
4. <u>*Be affectionate:*</u> I'm not talking about the bedroom. Tell your spouse that you love them. Those simple words, "I love you," when spoken in earnestness work miracles for each other. We still, after over 50 years of marriage, tell each other how much love we have for one another every day.
5. <u>*Show respect:*</u> Nothing destroys marriages quicker than a spouse who will not listen. Or, his/her opinion must come first. I have,

over years, counseled couples wherein one member of the family was totally tone deaf when it came to listening to the other's hurts. Selfish, self opinionated people seldom occupy a quality position in the marriage. Listening is not only a key element in marriage. It is everything! One of the key reasons for Jesus success in ministry was His ability to listen. The Gospels are filled with magnificent stories of Our Lord carefully listening to the cries of others.

6. *Seek counseling:* Seek outside counseling if you feel your marriage is in trouble. Sometimes a good outside friend can be of great aid; but seek counseling if you see your marriage caving in. There are a bevy of qualified people including your own pastor willing to help. Do not be a lone ranger, as too many times

they fall off their horse after being hit with verbal gunshot and harsh words are far more dangerous than steel bullets.

No person has ever been called to a God given mission without the anointing of His spirit to accomplish what he has been called to do. Sometimes, in order to deserve the workings of the Holy Sprit, a breaking must take place. In reading the history of Christ's Disciples one can see they went through great trials before becoming Christ orientated. During the "training period" he'll continually watch over you. This is why we were and continue to be protected. He'll do the same for you! You may not comprehend our words at this time. That is OK. Someday, before you check out of this world, you will. The Lord has promised me that all who read this book will eventually be changed.

We have two friends who are enduring great spiritual traumas on His behalf. They have chosen to follow Him verses engaging themselves in the secular world.

The first warrior for God is Bishop C. T. Wells, Senior Pastor of Emmanuel Church in Portland, Oregon. www.emmanuelpdx.com. I have know this Afro-American, Spiritual Crusader, for over 30 years. Several chapters could have easily been penned dedicated to the trials this servant of God has suffered under the umbrella of Wit's End. In all our years of fellowship I have never seen this champion deviate from the path God had planned for him. He is an inspiration to all he comes in contact with. Bishop C.T., with a Masters from George Fox University, is a trained writer and musical innovator. His gift on the keyboard, including the creating of music, could have easily produced for him untold sums of money in the outside world under the semblance of jazz or musical scores attributed to television programming associated with advertising and the like. His income today is still far below the national standard of Church Pastors. That however is secondary to him.

In spite of his familiarity with secular music, he chose to serve Our Lord as a preacher, teacher encourager, writer, counselor and church builder in that particular section of Portland known for its high crime activities.

I am moved to mention Bishop C.T.'s positive attitude which radiates solid confidence. Some people struggle to understand how to have a positive attitude when you're constantly threatened with outside forces attempting to pull down your obedience to Christ. Our Lord has given this leader a fixed positive frame of mind as a central gift in helping those who have lost jobs, failed at marriage or just bottomed out. One great characteristic of Bishop C.T. is his love of mankind. He has been Christ indentured with the love of Jesus for those who hurt.

I am futuristically predicting that you will hear much about this man of God who persists in knocking down enemy doors in spite of constant battles associated with Wit's End.

If your seeking a Church where God abides than you need not look any further. Emmanuel Church is located at 1033 North Sumner Street Portland, Oregon 97217. Phone 503.287.2223. The Church web site is www.emmanuelpdx.com.

The second is Pastor Tom Demaree of Memphis, Tennessee who founded Pentecost Walk. www.pentecostwalk.org or www.ru4one.com. Tom is one of the most talented people I have ever encountered.

His gift as a musical creator is uncanny. Without boasting Tom could easily have become a rock star [Piano man] Billy Joel. At one time, when Pastor Tom and I were in the Hilton Hotel—in San Diego—Tom took off on the piano that was located in the ground floor restaurant. Within seconds he had attracted crowds of people around him somewhat like that of bees charging honey. However, instead of entertaining the secular Tom transformed his musical creativeness to the glory of God. Over the past twenty years he and his wife Deanna have built one of the most dynamic, international ministries imaginable. Tom knows all too well about Wit's End. His family has suffered tremendously over the years from Churches and individuals who felt his gift was not for the 21st Century. There are times when Tom and I do not agree on the Ministerial path to be taken. Irrespective, Pastor Tom has grown mightily and prospered spiritually through Christ because of God's promises that "He would sanctify, encourage and protect Tom, in the midst of the storm." Tom's health has recently been tested in which he is currently on blood thinners. Yet this savant man of God presses on so as to answer God's calling. I encourage you to consider supporting this major ministry.

Epilogue

Many times I have said that I know God is real as I read the last chapter [Revelations] first. In simple terms, I know He is the beginning and the end. Or I do not classify myself a savant scholar. However I know our God is as real as the incandescent sun that shines in the heavens.

I know He physically exists due to the all too numerous miracles He has provided during my lifespan. Some of those marvelous and amazing events are defined within these pages.

So I'm totally entrenched within the framework of God. How do I maintain a close association with Him when the world we live in is crumbling around us including close calamities such as job loss, financial disparity, spouse wars, mind boggling children, chemistry disparities with supervisors, illness and depression to name a few?

First, we must understand and agree that things will never improve on this rock pile called earth. Our Lord has warned us that towards the end things would get worse and the only way you can deny this is in being a victim of too many day time TV soap operas.

WHAT IS WRONG

Scientists of the world, according to USA TODAY, NEWSWEEK and TIME, are more concerned than ever relative to our world's ever changing atmospheric. Simply put, things are drastic and these sweeping changes are all part of our end times as described by Our Lord. Here are some facts for you to ponder lest you think my thoughts are somewhat dysfunctional.

NEWSWEEK and TIME in their June, 2011 issues reported:

1. The litany of weather extremes has reached biblical proportions.
2. The 2010 heat wave killed an estimated 15,000 people in Russia.
3. Floods in Australia and Pakistan killed 2000 and left large swaths of land under water.

A month long drought in China has devastated million of acres of farmland and the temperature keeps rising.
2010 was the hottest year on earth ever since weather records begin.
The stable climate of the last 1200 years is gone. Those in the business of science technologies say we've seen nothing yet

as we'll shortly be facing more climate changes associated with disappearing islands in the Chesapeake and dust bowls in the Plains. This will also include more horrific [Joplin, Missouri] type tornadoes and—as a nation—are not ready.

November 2007 the Indian Council of Medical research (ICMR), along with several of the world's most renowned health scientists met to discuss the world's uncontrolled communicable diseases. Their report confirmed that chronic and non-communicable diseases are reaching world epidemic proportions. Diarrheal diseases alone kill millions yet nearly 1.1 billion people are lacking clean drinking water. A shortage of proper funding, wars to include idiotic Third World leaderships, keep Satan in business.

One could write pages of data relative to the challenges facing our own USA. However, you—as reader—are fully aware of the "uncontrolled and unchecked" problems facing a bankrupt, crime ridden country.

America would need to create 187,000 jobs a month, growing at a rate of 3.3% to get a healthy 5% unemployment rate by 2020.

The McKinsey Global Institute estimates it will take 60 months for jobs to return to prerecession levels this time around.

Half of Americans say they could not come up with $2000 in 30 days without selling some of their possessions.

Additionally—HARPER'S—in their "HARPER'S INDEX", reported that the minimum percentage of mortgages, in Las Vegas, Nevada, that are currently upside down is represented by a factor of 70 percent.

O America, your citizens and cities—once so very beautiful—have allowed her children to become involved with harlots so as to become harlots!

To put it simply, the USA is in for a mighty fall. It can be described through Ezekiel 7: 5, 8-9, 12, 17 and 27C which reads, "This is what the Sovereign Lord says: Disaster! An unheard of disaster is coming. (8) I am about to pour out my wrath and spread my anger against you; I will judge you according to your conduct and repay you for all your testable practices. (9) I will not look look on you with pity or spare you; I will repay you in accordance with your conduct and the detestable practices among you. Then you will know that it is I the LORD who strikes the blow. (12) The time has come, the day has arrived. Let not the buyer rejoice nor the seller grieve, for wrath is upon the whole crowd (17) Every hand will go limp, and every knee will become weak as water. (27C) Then they will know that I am the Lord." [NIV]

WHAT TO DO DURING THESE TIMES OF GREAT CLAMITY RELATIVE TO KEEPING YOUR FAMILY IN TACT

4. *<u>Listen to God:</u>* How? Continued Bible study followed by constant prayer and meditation. Pray when taking a shower, driving your car or at work. Pray when entering your bed; commence prayer before your feet hit the floor in the morning. You follow this pattern and Our Lord will talk to you on a regular basis. He'll tell you what to do and where not to go and with whom you should be in contact.
5. *<u>Be obedient to His will:</u>* One of the most powerful scriptures associated with this theme is found is Philippians 2: 5-6. "Let this mind be in you which was in Christ Jesus (6) Who, being in the form of God,

thought it not robbery to be equal with God." *In other words, let the mind of self-emptying be in you which was in Christ.* I know more about the effects of self emptying than most. Franklin was so bent, in years past, on his career that, although he was saved, his mind was deliriously bent on career success versus success through Our Lord. Thank God [literally] that He rescued me from a fall that was certain to take place. This is, putting your career in first place is the same as serving the Moabite idol, Baal-Peor. This foolishness will eventually lead to a painful downfall. Our Lord carefully tells us that we cannot serve two masters. A substantial numbers of you reading this book have a first position love affair with your Baal-peor be it your car, job, hobby, bank account or self.

Then, you have said, in your own words to God paradoxically, "O Lord. Make me into the kind of person pleasing to you." Believe me, He will. You had better hope that you're not in left field bowing down to your own Baal-peor when He comes calling. That is where I was when He said, "OK Franklin, I am coming to change your life by transporting you out of self. "

6. <u>*Be willing to pay the price:*</u> Matthew 16:26 reads "What good will it be for a man if he gains the Whole world, yet he forfeits his soul? Or what can a man give in exchange for his soul"? God has branded that verse into the frontlets of my lobe. I look back, in the days when I was chasing my career, better known as Franklin's Moabite idol, and realize that I have been rescued from a fate worse than an

incurable disease by Our Lord. I could have, if in refusing Our Lord, compiled substantial wealth. What, in the end would that have bought for me? Stool softeners, bifocals, canes, a body that had reached the state of immobility, meaningless business friends while looking forward to a bleak eternity due to my selfishness, pride and refusal to heed my Lord's calling along with the fact that I left my beautiful wife alone for so many years while chasing my spiritless idol. I have such compassion for the millions of Americans who are today where I was years ago. They are like lemmings following the same path in an attempt to find happiness. Yet with each day there remains emptiness and they know not why. Many fail in Him as they will not wait for His word to manifest itself. Without bragging or embellishment, I am one of the few who listened to Him before it was too late.

If my people, which are called by my name shall humble themselves and pray, and seek My face, and turn from their wicked ways, then I shall hear from heaven, and will forgive their sins, and will heal their land. II Chronicles 7:14 KJV

Can a mature Christian make a six figure income while remaining close to Christ? Yes, however, it is most difficult to accomplish. The more money you produce the more the world pushes you to press on for bigger and better "things". Your Moabite idol desires more such as bigger homes, fancier cars, more folding money in the pocket and of course the ever-loving Gold American Express Card with—due to good credit—no limit.

So what does a willingness to pay the price mean to today's Christian? It means your willingness to stay the course He has you on irrespective to storms of life; it means that during this short life your willing to give Him your time, talent and effort in exchange for a blissful eternity that you will share with billions of others who have gone before you; it means you have learned nothing is worth dying for, on this rock pile, unless He is leading the charge.

Well, I've reached the end. Anything else would most likely be repetitive. I humbly submit to you that I am not a prolific or professional writer so if you'll most likely find writer flaws.

The data you read herein is from my heart. What I did, how I did it, why I failed in business due to my not listening to Him, followed by Our Lord lifting me up again successfully (only) through the blessings and mercy of our Lord.

I wish you well, until we all cross over to the other side. I especially desire that you continue in excellent health and success through Christ who has called you to a better life.

I am more than pleased to dialogue with you or help assist you through any trial or complication that is currently encroaching your soul. Feel free to contact me through drfranklinaalvey@aol.com.

In respect,

Franklin

ACKNOWLEDGEMENTS

There are a group of people I feel exceptionally close to in addition to those already mentioned. These are individuals who have left an indelible impression on my life. They, on a daily basis, help me in my quest to be the proper bond servant to Our Lord.

Clayborn Collins, Ph.D.
> Dr. Collins is the Executive Director of Emmanuel Community Services which is an adjunct to Emmanuel Church. Seldom have I evidenced one with a sharper mind relative to mathematics and numbers in general. This former US Marine has an exceptional soft heart for your Lord. He has been a

keen ally to me and I believe Jesus has great plans for his future.

Rosemary Daniels, Ph.D.
I find it difficult to describe a person who is "always there." A individual who is continually giving, always witnessing, repeatedly encouraging, never taking down or failing their faith while volunteering more man hours to their Church than is possible to comprehend. This represents a segment of Dr. Daniels personality who also holds the position as treasurer of Emmanuel Church. If Churches, across America, had a handful of people like Rosemary Daniels, the attitude of our country would be changed to the positive.

Debra Kimbrough:
Seldom have I ever witnessed an individual more in love with Jesus

Christ than this woman. She is literally a giant among God's Saints. Debra, also married to a Pastor, is charged with overseeing all financial records for both Emmanuel Community Service and Emmanuel Church. The job at times is overwhelming due to the vastness of required reports to State and Governmental agencies. I have known this warrior for Christ since late 1970 and have witnessed her battle some of the most horrific spiritual wars, through tears, yet never to give an inch to the enemy.

Brad Stewart, Ph.D.

Dr. Brad is Director of Kingdom Warrior Men's Ministries including Director and overseer of (ISI) Iron Sharpens Iron whose mission is to resource local Churches with a first class one-day equipping conference that is specifically designated to pull men from shark infested sea of sin. It works! Dr. Brad has the responsibility in managing the ISI programs covering Oregon and Washington. This wonderful man, through his many men's conferences, has been responsible for introducing thousands of men to Christ. He is relentless in his pursuit to create as many participating men's gatherings as possible benefiting the Gospel. He earned his Doctorate after serving in the US Navy for more than 20 years. I am most pleased that he is my good friend. God is even more pleased that he is a first-rate friend to thousands of men who would not be in Christ if it were not for Dr. Brad's ministry.

SOURCES

1. Holy Bible quoted from KJV, NIV and RSV
2. The Movie, "Good night and good luck" directed by George Clooney
3. Abraham Lincoln
4. Bible History by Professor Alfred Eldersheim', Hendrickson Publishers by permission.
5. The movie, "The Edge'. A quote by actor Anthony Hopkins.
6. Don't waste your sorrows by Paul Billheimer; A Christian Literature Publications, by permission.
7. Coach Don Nava (www.coachin@thetotallyfitlife.com) By permission.
8. Michael Easley, Moody Bible Institute
9. Winston Churchill
10. USA TODAY
11. Center For The Bio Ethical Reform
12. www.thisistheendoftheworldasweknowit.com
13. National Oceanic and Atmospheric Administration
14. AOL

15. Consumer Report Magazine
16. The Oregonian
17. The United Nations Food and Agriculture Organization
18. CNN
19. FOX
20. The Economist
21. Charlie 'Tremendous" Jones
22. You Tube
23. Pastor E.R. Adebayo
24. C.T. Studd, "Cricketer & Pioneer" by Norman Grubb
25. Paul Harvey
26. Pastor Tom Demaree (www.pentecostalwalk.org) \
27. NEWSWEEK
28. TIME
29. ICMC
30. ICMR
31. McKinsey Global Institute
32. Harper's, "Harper's Index"
33. The Voice of the Martyrs
34. Bishop C.T. Wells

CPSIA information can be obtained at www.ICGtesting.com
Printed in the USA
270639BV00001B/1/P